TELETECHNIQUES

An Instructional Model for Interactive Teleconferencing

The Instructional Design Library

Volume 38

TELETECHNIQUES

An Instructional Model for Interactive Teleconferencing

Lorne A. Parker

University of Wisconsin-Extension
Madison, Wisconsin

and

Mavis K. Monson

University of Wisconsin-Extension
Madison, Wisconsin

Danny G. Langdon
Series Editor

Educational Technology Publications
Englewood Cliffs, New Jersey 07632

Library of Congress Cataloging in Publication Data

Parker, Lorne A
  Teletechniques, an instructional model for interactive teleconferencing.

  (The Instructional design library; v. 38)
  Bibliography: p.
  1. Teleconferencing in education. 2. Forums
(Discussion and debate) I. Monson, Mavis K., joint
author. II. Title. III. Series: Instructional
design library; v. 38.
LB1044.9.T38P37   371.3'7   79-24442
ISBN 0-87778-158-3

LB
1044.9
.T38
P37
1980

Printed in the United States of America.

Library of Congress Catalog Card Number:
79-24442.

International Standard Book Number:
0-87778-158-3.

First Printing: March, 1980.

FOREWORD

This book demonstrates that the telephone can be an effective and efficient medium for the delivery of instruction, using formats which go well beyond the lecture approach.

The authors concentrate on the instructional design components of telephone-based instruction, including how to assure that learning is taking place.

Readers will appreciate the manner in which the authors have organized their presentation, especially the "hip pocket" techniques and the illustrative materials showing key aspects of humanizing instruction, assuring participation, message style, and feedback.

With the ever-growing nature of continuing professional education, special learning needs, and the call for lifelong learning in all areas of society, the designs discussed in this book are to be welcomed as significant contributions.

Danny G. Langdon
Series Editor

PREFACE

During the past 20 years, technological equipment more glamorous than the telephone has dominated educational media. Yet, because it is interactive, low-cost, and effective, many institutions are refocusing attention on the telephone to meet rising educational and training demands. There have been studies of telephone courses for credit, teacher education, extension courses, on-the-job training sessions, and even art education with the aid of overhead transparencies. These studies indicated that education using telephone technology is effective.

The University of Wisconsin-Extension program began its Educational Telephone Network (ETN) in 1965 to provide quality, low-cost, continuing education to physicians in their home communities. From the original 18 sites, the interactive network now encompasses Wisconsin's 72 counties with 200 separate ETN classrooms. More than 200 program series are offered each year. Classroom settings include county courthouses, hospital board rooms, and libraries, as well as campus facilities. More than 35,000 people, representing a variety of occupations, participate annually.

The technology is simple to use and requires no special skills. Although the transmission system consists of telephone lines, the "telephone network" station equipment no longer resembles a telephone handset. Instead, each of the classrooms has a suitcase-size speaker, which plugs into a standard telephone jack and AC power outlet, and four microphones.

When participants press a bar on the base of a microphone and speak, their questions or comments are heard by all statewide participants. The network interconnections use approximately 5,000 miles of voice channels and the services of 20 telephone companies to provide the statewide coverage.

But successful hardware or technical systems cannot in themselves guarantee successful usage of an interactive network such as ETN. Critical to the operation of a successful delivery system are the design and implementation of software or course content that is specific to the interactive audio medium. This book presents a model for designing teleconferencing programs.

L.A.P.
M.K.M.

CONTENTS

ABSTRACT

TELETECHNIQUES

The Teletechniques instructional design is a model for two-way interactive teleconferencing. It provides a framework in which to design effective educational programs in a variety of teleconferencing contexts. Teleconferencing is a unique medium which allows groups or individuals to interact from distant locations using telecommunications technology, which can range from simple telephone handsets to sophisticated speaker/microphone units. Messages can be sent down ordinary telephone lines or via microwave, cable, or satellite links.

The Teletechniques design can be applied to a wide range of teleconferencing applications, for example: *telelecture* (a resource person instructing a class via amplified telephone to provide expertise that would otherwise not be available) or *telephone-based instruction* (an educational program offered to groups or individuals at many locations by an instructor at another location with all participants interacting on a huge "party line").

Underlying assumptions about the teleconferencing environment which relate to the Teletechniques model are:

- individuals are physically distant from one another;
- individuals are using telecommunications technology to interact with one another;
- individuals may not be accustomed to the technology;

- individuals may be participating with a group or may be all alone at the various locations; and
- in audio conferencing, the visual element is not available.

There are four components to the Teletechniques design. Each step is important in maximizing the use of the medium. (1) *Humanizing*—the process of creating an atmosphere which focuses on the importance of each individual and overcomes a feeling of distance by generating a "one group" rapport. (2) *Participation*—the process of getting beyond the technology by providing opportunities for (and encouragement of) spontaneous interaction between students as well as the instructors. (3) *Message Style*—the process of presenting a message in such a way so as to increase the chances that what is said will be received, understood, and remembered. (4) *Feedback*—the process of getting back information about the message which helps both the teacher and the student complete the communications loop, to help in correcting misunderstandings and filling in omissions.

TELETECHNIQUES

An Instructional Model for Interactive Teleconferencing

I.

USE

The Teletechniques instructional design was developed to meet the needs of individuals who are involved in the planning, implementation, and evaluation of teleconferencing, for meetings and/or instruction. Teleconferencing is still a rather new concept to many people, so before beginning a discussion of Teletechniques, perhaps the word "teleconferencing" should be defined and its use in education more fully detailed. Teleconferencing means interactive group communication using an electronic medium. The word "interactive" is important in this definition because it emphasizes that the communication is two-way, allowing for exchanges between individuals. The "electronic medium" mentioned in the definition might be audio (for example, the use of a telephone system) or it might be video or computer. There are as many teleconferencing configurations as there are instructional uses for it.

Teleconferencing in Instruction

The first instructional use of teleconferencing that we know about was in Iowa in 1939. Telephone "intercom devices" were installed to allow homebound and hospitalized students to communicate with their classrooms. Class lectures were transmitted to the students simultaneously as they were presented to the classroom students. Teacher and students

were able to talk with the homebound pupils. The first
college level application was at the University of Illinois
College of Dentistry in 1947. Six lectures were transmitted to
30 dentists in Scranton, Pennsylvania, and they were given to
50 dentists in a classroom on the Chicago campus. These
lectures-by-phone, or "telelectures" as they were called, used
a simple device known as an "amplified telephone," which
was basically a telephone hooked into an amplifier-speaker-
microphone arrangement. The unit allowed large groups of
students to hear and talk with the remote instructor.

It wasn't until the 1960's that full scale "networks" of
classrooms came into existence. Using newly developed
bridging techniques, groups at many locations could be
linked together for instructional classes or administrative
meetings. Equipment in the classrooms was still simple to
operate, albeit a much more sophisticated amplifier-speaker-
microphone unit.

Currently, teleconferencing, when thought of in a broad
context, is an umbrella term which covers many other
options in equipment, linkages, and transmission systems. It
can range from the simple "amplified phone call" described
above to full video conferencing. It can include computer
conferencing. It can refer to systems which use telephone
lines to transmit the signals or to systems which use satellite
links. There are, fortunately, certain underlying assumptions
which are common to all teleconferencing environments,
whether audio, video, or computer, that allow us to apply
some of the same instructional design strategies. We might
note, however, that Teletechniques was originally designed
with an audio teleconference in mind, so when we use the
word "teleconferencing" in the design model, we are refer-
ring to an interactive audio system.

Most of the audio teleconferencing being done in the
world today is via telephone lines using telephone technology. Although the telephone is no longer a startling

innovation in communication, it has been only in the past few years that several technological advances have made it one of the more flexible means of instruction in distant learning education. Use of the telephone as a tool for interactive instruction is still a relatively new concept. It is a way of helping those unable or unwilling to participate in traditional learning activities by bringing resource people not ordinarily available right into their own community classroom.

Perhaps the best way to begin learning about how audio teleconferencing is used in instruction would be to define and illustrate some of the more common ways it is utilized in educational settings today:

Telelecture is a prearranged phone call from a classroom to a resource person to enrich regular classroom instruction by bringing in expertise that would otherwise not be available. Telelecture provides students the opportunity to ask questions and make comments which are amplified through special telephone equipment for the entire classroom. To make it more convenient for students to interact with the resource person, several microphones may be placed in various locations throughout the room.

One high school's telelecture program uses telelectures in history, English, social studies, and journalism classes. The journalism class uses them to teach students how to research a topic. Students selected for interviewing guest speakers first read and research the subject, then carefully plan questions for the interview. The telelectures are particularly useful in career-oriented classes because they enable students to talk with people who work in various fields. Recent telelectures included interviews with the U.S. ambassador to West Germany, author Pearl Buck, comedian Alan King, and author Isaac Asimov.

Teleteaching enables a sick or handicapped student at home to keep up with the class without actually being present through the use of a two-way telephone placed in the classroom. The student can hear all that is going on in the class via the teleconferencing equipment and can indicate by a signal when he or she wants to speak or answer a question. Everyone in the classroom is able to hear what he or she says, as if the student were present in the classroom.

One state's "home-to-school" service is a program where selected classrooms are fitted with special telephone sets. A high school girl so crippled by cerebral palsy that she could not be in the classroom was successfully taught typewriting using portable conferencing equipment for the instruction.

Teletutoring gives students a means of getting in touch with a teacher or tutor for individual help. Used mainly in correspondence education or other types of independent study, the teletutoring can originate with a call from the student to the tutor or vice-versa. Teletutoring can also be used for tutorial groups with individuals located at several locations.

The British Open University uses teletutoring on a group basis, where a number of groups are connected by telephone to discuss course work. The course work may be delivered by a variety of methods: correspondence, textbooks, television, or radio programs. Teletutoring allows students to get immediate feedback in answering questions and solving problems related to the actual course work, and to overcome a feeling of being isolated as an independent learner when participating in mediated instruction.

Telewriting is the use of a visual component to supplement audio teleconferencing. This visual component can be used with all phases of teleconferencing. Telewriting uses a device, either mechanical-electronic or fully electronic, which enables an instructor to send hand-drawn graphics down the telephone lines. The graphics portion of the message is then reproduced at the remote locations via an overhead projection system or on a television monitor, depending on the system used.

One state system which uses a telewriting device (in combination with a teleconferencing network of over 20 locations) has successfully taught engineering courses for over ten years to hundreds of professionals wishing to continue their education. Courses are provided in civil, electrical, and mechanical engineering, mathematics, computer science, mechanics, and minerals and metallurgical engineering.

Telephone-based instruction uses a system which transmits and amplifies the communications between an instructor and groups of students or single individuals at distant locations. The system might be thought of as a huge "party line" where all groups and individuals can hear and interact with each other. This allows questions, discussion, and other participation by everyone. Telephone-based instructional systems can be "dedicated" (a permanently installed network) or "dial-up" (a network established at the time the class is held).

Over the past 13 years, a large state system has given a broad array of course offerings using a network of over 200 locations. Basically delivering continuing and adult education programs, the network has more than 200 course offerings each year. Topics include agriculture, business, engineering, health and medicine, home economics, music, communications and journalism, library science, and continuing education for attorneys.

From the illustrations above, you can see that the use of teleconferencing falls into three basic categories:

1. *Course enrichment.* Telelectures bring into the class-room resource persons who would otherwise not be available. Teleconferencing is not an integral but an occasional function.
2. *Integral part but combined with other learning modes.* Teleconferences used in a media mix situation where face-to-face sessions, television or videotapes, and teleconferences are combined. Teleconferencing is used as an integral part of the total instructional plan.
3. *Sole instruction.* Teleconferences are used as the delivery mechanism for the entire instructional load.

Meeting Student and Teacher Needs

Teleconferencing used as an alternative educational method providing the third function (sole instruction) prospers in areas where it meets very real, pragmatic, professional, and economic needs. The lawyer who continually needs to keep abreast of changes in the law in order to maintain his or her license; the doctor whose constant needs to continue his or her education are juxtaposed against his or her need to stay near the community he or she serves; the librarian who has 150 miles and a harsh winter climate separating him or her and the nearest degree-granting campus . . . and the instructors who, because of professional commitments and the sheer logistics of limited time and economics, cannot serve a statewide clientele in traditional face-to-face methods.

The University of Wisconsin-Extension's ETN

An example of how teleconferencing has flourished because of meeting these real, pragmatic needs is the University of Wisconsin-Extension's Educational Telephone Network (ETN), currently the largest, most sophisticated teleconferencing system in the United States. It started in 1965 with 18 listening sites around the state of Wisconsin. Because of the primitive state-of-the-art of station equipment and bridging techniques, listeners might hear a lecture quite clearly one minute, then nothing but static the next. While it was up to the telephone company to work out the technical details, it was up to the University of Wisconsin-Extension faculty, program facilitators, and instructional designers to work out the program details.

The first program was a seminar for physicians, a group that needed classes in order to learn the latest medical knowledge but couldn't afford the time to travel far from their patients. This first class was a success and the Educational Telephone Network was on its way. The next year, three new health programs were scheduled and the decision was to start programs for other professionals. Lawyers, for instance, attended ETN noon lectures while they ate their sack lunches. Over the years, they had one of the highest turnouts of any group, about 500 per program.

Soon programs were offered to the general public as well as professionals. Programs included law for the layman, a course on venereal disease, a discussion of the effects of television violence on children, and another on how to be a better homemaker. Most classes were non-credit, although some credit courses were offered each semester.

In recent years, the Educational Telephone Network has offered classes in photography and music. In Photo Fundamentals, for example, students mailed in their class assignments to their instructor, who critiqued and returned them.

At present, there are over 200 University of Wisconsin-Extension courses offered each year to more than 35,000 students.

How Versatile Is Teleconferencing?

We have briefly described the University of Wisconsin-Extension system with its broad range of course offerings.

The range of potential applications of teleconferencing appears to be limited only by the imagination, interest, and motivation of those instructing the courses. Teleconferencing has been successfully used with many ages of learners: elementary, high school, college, and adults. It has been used at various levels of learner sophistication. It has been used successfully in both formal and informal instructional situations. It has been used to teach courses in which the visual element would be considered to be an essential part of the instruction by supplementing it with overhead transparencies or slides in such subject matter areas as art, photography, and medicine. It has been used in courses which are heavily involved with complex psychomotor skills, for example, piano technique and cello bowing technique.

Expanding the Uses of Teleconferencing

Teleconferencing will continue to play an important role in education. The uses described above are within a *narrow* educational context. Within a *broad* context, teleconferencing's role extends beyond the types of functions we described above to include many "noninstructional" or related uses. These noninstructional uses increase the utilization and cost-efficiency of a teleconferencing system. Administrative uses, information exchanges, and interorganizational context are just a few examples.

Administrative Uses

At the Wisconsin network, administrative uses include statewide meetings, a message service, and information exchanges. One morning a week, for example, Extension faculty and staff participate in a statewide meeting conducted by the Community Programs Department. Every weekday morning, messages from the University Extension Office in Madison are relayed to faculty around the state. Immediately following this exchange, the traffic is reversed, allowing agents to forward messages to the Madison office. Immediately following this message service each morning, the system is reserved for 15 minutes so that county extension agents can confer with each other. Sometimes they make prior arrangements for their discussion, but more often than not you can hear a faculty member such as Herman Smith say, "This is Smith in Oneida County. Is Merrill on the line?" The chances are pretty good that Merrill *is* on the line, and Smith gets his message through.

Information Exchanges

Among its other uses, the ETN system links regional faculties for information exchanges. It also links 4-H Club activities, and it provides county Extension faculty an opportunity to exchange weekly information with agricultural specialists. ETN has also been used to disseminate emergency information to agricultural agents. An outbreak of corn yellow leaf blight on Wisconsin farms brought an Extension plant pathologist to the telephone network with information for agricultural agents on the status of the disease and recommendations for its control.

Interorganizational Context

An example of how the network was used within an "interorganizational context" would be a program designed for clergy. Sharing of the program for clergy in Kansas, as well as Wisconsin, was accomplished through a link between the two networks. Thus, course sharing and exchange of research and educational resources among organizations serving similar goals is a use of a teleconferencing system that is now a reality.

The Future

The potentials that exist for even greater uses are there, waiting to be tapped. We have discussed the use of teleconferencing for "teletutoring." In independent study courses, there is a special need for this type of interaction, which extends over and beyond clarification of problems relating directly to subject matter by providing student-to-student exchange of communication to provide peer support outside of regular class work. However, teleconferencing could also provide student services in the form of sessions to help students deal with registration, procedures, and other common problems related to, but not directly part of, course material. Counseling by teleconference using "returning back to school" sessions might help those who have "stopped out" of the course progression.

The Rationale Behind Teletechniques

As is readily apparent, the development of the role that teleconferencing can play as an educational medium has just begun. Both direct instruction as well as related uses will continue to grow as the demand for effective, low-cost, readily available communication channels increases. However, successful teleconferencing programs consist of more than merely placing a microphone in a traditional face-to-face classroom situation and sending the spoken material out over telephone lines. The successfully developed telephone-taught course employs a number of teaching strategies designed specifically for this two-way audio medium. Thus, Teletechniques as a design model grew from the need for a simple, conceptual framework to incorporate these strategies. Teletechniques provides the tools to design effective teleconferencing programs across many disciplines and clientele groups.

References

Ahlm, M. Telephone Instruction in Correspondence Education. *Epistolodidaktika*, 1972, *2*, 49-64.

Duhrels, M. I Taught Typing by Telephone. *Business Education World,* April 1965, *16.*

Flinck, R. *Correspondence Education Combined with Systematic Telephone Tutoring.* Hermads: Sweden, 1978.

Jackson, L.B., L.A. Parker, and C.H. Olgren. Teleconferencing + Telewriting = Continuing Engineering Education in Wisconsin. *Technical Design for Audio Teleconferencing,* University of Wisconsin-Extension, Madison, Wisconsin, 1978.

Johansen, R., M. McNulty, and B. McNeal. *Electronic Education: Using Teleconferencing in Postsecondary Organizations.* Menlo Park, California: Institute for the Future, 1978.

Mandelbaum, J.D. Six Experimental Telelecture Sites Report. *Educational Screen and Audio Visual Guide,* May 1966, 32-33.

Parker, L.A., M. Baird, and D. Gilbertson. Introduction to Teleconferencing. *The Telephone in Education Book II,* University of Wisconsin-Extension, Madison, Wisconsin, 1977.

Rao, P.V., and B.L. Hicks. Telephone-Based Instruction Systems. *Audiovisual Instruction,* April 1972.

Rookey, E.J., L.W. Gill, and F.J. Gill. An Educational Telephone Network. *Educational Technology,* December 1971.

Steele, M.A. Teleteaching: A New Form of Home and Hospital Instruction. *Audiovisual Instruction,* November 1969.

Wrightstone, J.W. *et al. Evaluation of a Method of School-to-Home Telephone Instruction of Physically Handicapped Homebound Adolescents.* New York: Board of Education for the City of New York, 1968.

II.

OPERATIONAL DESCRIPTION

Development of an Instructional Design Strategy

Teletechniques is a set of guidelines or basic design components to be used in designing teleconferencing programs. It provides a framework in which to develop effective educational programs in a variety of teleconferencing modes. It is the purpose of this chapter to briefly and basically explain how Teletechniques works and how it fits into the overall instructional design sequence. (The instructional design sequence implies a systematic way of designing instructional experiences. There is no magic to the systems approach—it simply means a problem-solving process which is subdivided into practical, operational steps.) Within this overall design sequence, then, we would find Teletechniques to be part of a total instructional design system. That would include a number of instructional strategies that are integral to working with faculty, program facilitators, instructional designers, and learners in the teleconferencing environment. We will include in our discussion more about the instructional design model using the systems approach, but let us first look at the Teletechniques design components and how they operate.

Teletechniques was developed by studying both theory and practice. Theories of listening, learning, communications, and the psychology of distant learning environments, as well as the research in teleconferencing, formed a data base. These data were used along with the "hands-on" experience of teleconference instructors—instructors who had planned, implemented, and evaluated scores of successful teleconference programs. We learned that, although teleconferencing and face-to-face classes are in many ways the same, they differ, as one might intuitively suppose, in some others. The unique characteristics of the teleconferencing environment which relate to the Teletechniques design are:

- individuals are physically distant from one another;
- individuals are using telecommunications technology to interact with one another;
- individuals may not be accustomed to this technology, know how to operate it, nor feel comfortable in its initial use;
- individuals may be participating in a group situation or may be all alone at their locations; and,
- in audio teleconferencing, individuals cannot see one another as they communicate.

These characteristics of the teleconferencing environment provide some basic guidelines to use in thinking about instructional design for this medium. For example:

1. *Listening "groups" aren't always a group.*
   When one hundred students are dispersed geographically at some ten to 20 locations, it is difficult to make the listening groups a "group" and not just a collection of strangers. "Getting to know someone" in teleconferencing is not as easily accomplished as in a face-to-face setting.

2. *Discussion doesn't just "happen."*
   No matter how many students may want to make use of the opportunity to ask questions and no matter how easy it may be technically, some students are reluctant to interact at first—they may feel they are infringing on program time, other people's time, or

that their questions or comments may not be worded correctly.

3. *People don't listen very long.*
   It is hard work concentrating on a solitary audio message for very long. For adults, that "very long" is not much more than 12-15 minutes. For children, the time is shorter.

4. *Communication isn't complete until we get feedback.*
   In any communication with others, we haven't completed the loop until we can see that the message has been received and understood in the way we intended. In teleconferencing, non-verbal cues are not available as a feedback mechanism.

Thus, the teleconferencing environment is different from a face-to-face setting. In many cases, an effective teacher in a face-to-face setting will intuitively adapt successfully to teleconferencing. This person will recognize that many communication techniques that work well in a classroom may not be as successful in a teleconference. For example, many instructors are accustomed to giving 50 minutes of straight lecture, which when presented in a lively manner, will hold the students' attention. The same lecture, given over a sound-only medium, would probably not be as successful. Here the information must be adapted "for the ear." Presenting information, encouraging student participation, judging whether the message is getting across, and making sure that students feel a part of the group, even though separated by distance from the instructor, are some of the considerations for which an effective teleconferencing teacher must plan.

Thus, based on what we have learned about teleconferencing through research and practical experiences of instructors, a number of design elements have emerged. These design elements are tools to use when thinking about the design of a program for a two-way audio system. The four components are:

- HUMANIZING
- PARTICIPATION
- MESSAGE STYLE
- FEEDBACK

In the following chapter, we will discuss how these components can be operationalized on a practical level; but, at this point, we will define what they are and some of the ways these steps are used in an overall instructional strategy.

What Is Humanizing and Why Plan for It?

Humanizing is the process of creating an atmosphere which focuses on the importance of the individual and overcomes distance by generating group rapport. It is important to add humanizing to your list of planning considerations because many participants may be all alone at their locations; may never have used teleconferencing equipment before; and may be expecting something quite different from the teleconferencing experience. Humanizing techniques let individuals know that, although separated from you by great distances, their needs are important.

What Is Participation and Why Plan for It?

Participation in teleconferencing might be defined as the process of getting beyond the technology by providing opportunities for spontaneous interaction among participants. It is important to encourage involvement in the communications process, and it is important to plan time for these opportunities. One of the strengths of teleconferencing is its capability for two-way communication, and providing participation opportunities helps individuals maintain interest and commitment to the program.

What Is Message Style and Why Plan for It?

Message style is presenting what is to be said in such a way that it will be received, understood, and remembered. In teleconferencing, where participants are receiving the message by listening, it is important to think about the things we know with regard to listening that may help to improve the communications process. Certainly, there are some factors about listening yet to be discovered, but there are guidelines about presenting aural messages which can make presentations via teleconferencing more effective and enjoyable.

What Is Feedback and Why Plan for It?

Feedback is the process of getting information about the message which helps you and the participants complete the communications loop. It helps in correcting misunderstandings and filling in omissions. Feedback can also be used in planning future programs. It is important to consider how you will get feedback, because teleconferencing settings give you verbal cues only. With group members physically separated from you, you will want to find ways to get feedback during program time as well as off-the-air.

Ways of Using the Steps of Teletechniques

The four components described above—Humanizing, Participation, Message Style, and Feedback—are the basis for the Teletechniques model. The model has purposely been kept simple in concept and in operation. Teleconferencing cuts across subject matter areas, lengths of programs, types of student groups, sizes of audiences, and numbers of programs within a given course. For example, instructors may be full-time faculty, or they may be resource persons (brought into the network by phone from their home or studio many miles distant) who have expertise in their field but not necessarily in teaching methodology. Instructors who use the system may use it for a series of programs meeting a full semester, or they may have a single program each year.

Thus, to reach faculty with information about Teletechniques must necessarily take many forms. Three-hour workshops are given for interested faculty, a number of printed materials both capsulized and in-depth have been developed, and a very simple brochure is available to send to resource persons who, because of distances involved, cannot attend a workshop and also might not read a very large amount of print material. This many-pronged approach to implementing the model has been conceived with the idea of reaching faculty where they are.

"Hands-on" Method of Implementing Teletechniques Model

For those faculty who have both the time and interest in attending a three-hour workshop, the "hands-on" approach to learning proves to be most beneficial. Workshop attendees (program instructors or coordinators) are asked to assume roles of distant learners. Using a simulated teleconferencing network with a number of locations, the "distant learners" interact using the very type of equipment which is at each classroom around the state. Content presented over the simulated network by the workshop leaders is the Teletechniques model and its applications.

Evaluations of the workshop by attendees have shown that this "learning by doing" is effective and well received by faculty members. Not only does the "hands-on" experience allow the participants a chance to become acquainted and accustomed to working with microphones, but also it gives them the chance to experience what a distant learning environment is like—stimulating them to think creatively in adapting their programs to this medium.

Recently we have begun to use the network itself to provide training to groups or individuals who are unable to come to Madison. Using the medium to teach the medium is an exciting challenge and one that constantly stimulates us to improve on the existing training program. We want to keep the model simple, but effective. We recognize that Teletechniques is but a smaller part of a bigger picture. Teletechniques is a set of guidelines for working within a given instructional experience using teleconferencing. It is not intended to be an overall instructional design model. (It is important to note here that it is assumed that instructors who give programs over the system have an underlying framework or instructional design within which they are working.)

The Parker Instructional Design Model

If we wish to look at an overall systematic method of designing educational experiences using mediated instruction, one model is the Parker Instructional Design Model shown in Figure 1. There have been, in the past, many program design models. However, one feature most of them lack is the utilization of media research as an integral part of the decision-making process. For example, in the design process of an instructional sequence for television, the designer may leave out the crucial step of using the research which applies to the best utilization of television. Or, to take this a step further, the criteria for selecting television as a medium initially may not have been based on the research applicable to the subject. Possibly much instructional design which involves media is actually done by "intuition." This haphazard approach may be explained when we realize some of the factors involved: (1) research is not well publicized or in some cases not very credible, and (2) the media selection step has been left out or neglected in most design models.

Importance of the Research Matrix

The six steps in the Instructional Design Model are similar to other instructional design models—with one crucial difference: the addition of a research matrix. This matrix has three dimensions relating to media research. For the purpose of this model, *media* refers to any and all physical means of representing the entire set of stimulus conditions required in

Figure 1

The Parker Instructional Design Model

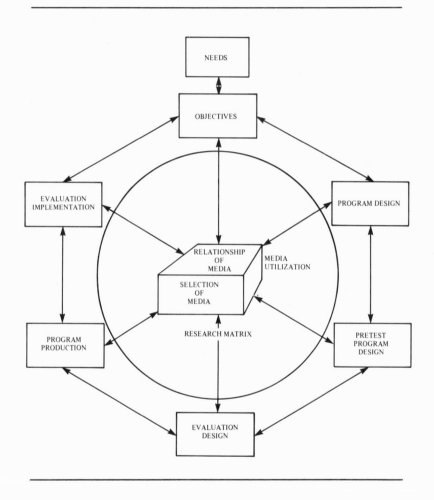

the instruction of a learner. Thus, media includes printed communications (books), oral communications (teachers), actual objects (realia), and special devices and materials (television, film, teaching machines, radio, slide-tapes, etc.).

The first dimension of the research matrix is to store information relative to the *selection* of the best media to accomplish a given objective. Within the matrix, information would be found on when to use television, teachers, lectures, or field trips, etc.

The second dimension would answer the question of how to *utilize* the media. For example, how many concepts should be transmitted, or the type of visuals, how long the presentation should be, the arrangement of feedback, and physical facilities. These are only some of the considerations in this phase of the matrix.

The third dimension involves media and their *relationship* to each other. Within this dimension, not only the relationship of media, but also the relationship of students and content should be considerations.

Operationalizing the Instructional Design Model

1. *Needs Phase*

   The first step is to state the need—the real need of the group under consideration. The real need should address the overall problem to be solved, not just the educational problem—for the first thing that must be considered is that instruction, in itself, may be just one solution to the problem. For example, a statement of the need should be: "We must provide better medical care," not: "We need a programmed instruction booklet series for nurses' training."

2. *Objectives Phase*

   Once the need is properly stated, we can determine

what learning objectives must be attained to satisfy the need. In this step, we decide what the student should be able to do after having completed the learning experience. This is an important step of the instructional design model, because all subsequent steps are designed to develop the learning experiences to meet these objectives. Hence, if the objectives are stated improperly, the learning experiences will not lead to the desired outcome. We must think in terms of an ends-centered as contrasted with a means-centered approach in this phase.

3. *Program Design Phase*

This phase deals with matching learning experiences to the expressed stated objectives which are related to the student's educational needs. Identifying the type of learning is the first step involved in this phase. Such criteria as the effectiveness, the time within which it could be completed, the degree of risk involved, and the total impact on other learning experiences should be considered. Here the research matrix is used to select the proper medium for the required learning experience. The matrix helps determine if a medium is applicable to a particular learning situation.

4. *Pretest Program Design Phase*

By pretesting the prescribed learning experiences and media on a typical sample audience, the content specialist and program designer are able to evaluate the various educational media selected out of the research matrix.

5. *Evaluation Design Phase*

In this phase, the type of evaluation instrument which will be used to measure the program design and educational objectives is developed. It is then tested in the Pretest Program-Instructional Design Phase. If the instrumentation is not functional or does not measure and supply criteria for the program designer and content specialist to make judgments, it will be necessary to use the research matrix to provide information for a redesign of the evaluation instrument.

6. *Program Production Phase*

This might also be called the "program presentation" phase. This phase brings together the integration of media. The term "production" is used to emphasize the aspect of planning time for the proper production of various media. Many programs have failed not because of poor design but because the design could not be utilized due to lack of production time.

7. *Evaluation Implementation Phase*

In the evaluation phase (the instrumentation having been evaluated for validity and reliability), the final results can be used to measure whether the objectives initially stated for the program have been achieved. Basically, there are two concerns in this phase. First, to measure the effectiveness of the *program design*. Secondly, from the criteria, to make judgments as to the total *design process.* For example, from the point of view of the design, this phase is important to judge whether or not learning took place. From the point of view of the process, judgments can be made as to whether a learning "environment" was created, and to what degree the program influenced its students. These judgments might suggest corrections in the program and alternatives for other programs.

Example of the Parker Instructional
Design Model in Operation

To illustrate the utilization of the research matrix, let us use an example with a broad objective: the needs of doctors in the state to receive continuing education in their home communities. This objective could be translated into the form of educational experiences. For example, one specific terminal objective within the broad objective might be: to allow doctors in the state to interact with a leading heart specialist located in South Africa.

This objective is then matched with the information we have about this input objective—using the research matrix. The matrix will allow us to select the media or medium that will meet the needs of this specific objective.

What might be the output of the matrix? It might suggest the selection of the medium of television with a two-way connection to the doctor in South Africa. But if we are working with a limited budget, this medium cannot be selected. We again go back to the research matrix. This time, a telephone conference call via satellite is suggested. Each doctor could participate in his or her local community and interact with the heart specialist in South Africa.

So far, the matrix has performed only one function—the selection of the proper medium for the needed learning experience.

The next step for the matrix system would be to provide information on the utilization of the medium. This phase would answer such questions as, "How long should the lecture or discussion be?" "How many doctors should be at one location?" "How should the room be organized?" "Should the program be pre-structured?" "What should the structure of the program be?" "Should each listening location have a moderator, and if so, how should he or she be trained?" "What is the moderator's role?"

The third dimension will answer questions regarding the

relationship of media. For this particular illustration, there would be very little relationship. But to expand the illustration, suppose the matrix also indicated that visual information should accompany the telephone lecture. Slides or pictures could be supplied to each listening location. Thus, we have a media relationship. The matrix would produce studies that indicate that two "channels," such as audio and visual, should complement one another. For example, when emphasizing the visual, the audio is silent, allowing time for the eye to record the visual message. Conversely, if the message is via audio, use of a primary color visual will help emphasize the audio message. Thus, the color slide or visual serves as a mental switching device and cues the appropriate human sensory channel.

In summary, the instructional design model provides a research matrix which stores information on three dimensions: (1) the selection of the proper media for the needed learning experience, (2) information on how to utilize the media, and (3) information on how various media interrelate with each other. Using the research matrix can serve to strengthen the decision-making process in the planning and implementation of instructional programs.

References

Allen, W. Instructional Media Research: Past, Present, Future. *AV Communication Review,* Spring 1971, 5-18.

Cooley, W.W., and R.C. Hummel. System Approaches in Guidance. *Review of Educational Research, 39,* 251-261.

Fine, T.W. Implementing a Needs Assessment Program. *Educational Technology,* February 1969, 30-31.

Kaufman, R., and F.W. English. *Needs Assessment: Concept and Application.* Englewood Cliffs, New Jersey: Educational Technology Publications, 1979.

Lehmann, H. The Systems Approach to Education. *Audiovisual Instruction,* February 1968, 144-148.

Severin, W. The Effectiveness of Relevant Pictures in Multiple-Channel Communications. *A V Communication Review,* Winter 1967.

Travers, R.M.W. *Research and Theory Related to Audiovisual Information Transmission.* Washington, D.C.: U.S. Office of Education, Contract No. OES-16-006.

III.

DESIGN FORMAT

The Teletechniques design consists of four parts:
- HUMANIZING
- PARTICIPATION
- MESSAGE STYLE
- FEEDBACK

These four parts or steps are used as groupings under which to coordinate the practical techniques; techniques which are used to provide for more effective, satisfying teleconferencing. The four steps provide a framework in which to think about the characteristics of the teleconferencing environment described in the Operational Description chapter and summarized below:

- "Listening groups aren't always a 'group'."
- "Discussion doesn't always just happen."
- "People don't listen very long."
- "The communications loop isn't complete until we get feedback."

The four steps are intentionally simple in their concept, as well as in their application. It is important that a *programmer** new to teleconferencing is not overwhelmed with

---

*The term *programmer* will be used in this guide to identify any individual who may play a role in the design of a teleconference— whether in the role of instructor, moderator, coordinator, or instructional designer.

procedural "do's" and "don't's" in using the medium for the first time. The strategy is to make teleconferencing appealing. It is a challenge, of course, to one's creative abilities to develop successful teleconferences, but a challenge that can be enjoyable and in which it is possible to have successes right from the start. (In comparison with other types of media, teleconferencing is relatively simple to program.)

We might also note that many of the suggested practices may be regarded at first glance as "obvious" or "just plain common sense." They are, admittedly, in their simplicity, common sense rules-of-thumb. However, one of the reasons many of these practices are overlooked the first time by instructors is because *they are so obvious,* so taken for granted in a face-to-face setting. For example, under FEED-BACK, it is suggested that every comment made by a student should be *acknowledged* by a *verbal comment* from the instructor to help communication flow. This might seem to be a common-sense statement. However, in a face-to-face setting, acknowledgment might be by a nod of the head or a shrug of the shoulders—very unconscious, spontaneous gestures. In teleconferencing, these cues would not be available to the student, thus, acknowledgment by a *verbal* cue from the instructor takes on great importance.

Before going into greater detail about each component, its importance in teleconferencing, and how to operationalize it, let us once again define each step:

- HUMANIZING is the creation of an environment which emphasizes the importance of the individual and which overcomes any barriers of distance by generating a feeling of group rapport.
- PARTICIPATION is transcending technological factors to allow a more natural interaction to take place by providing for and encouraging opportunities to communicate on the part of participants.
- MESSAGE STYLE is planning the information in

such a way that what is said will be received, understood, and remembered by the participants.

- FEEDBACK is getting the information that is necessary to enable both speaker and listener to correct errors and omissions and to help improve future communications by completing the communications "loop."

Humanizing in Teleconferencing

One of the main ways of beginning to humanize is to establish some type of personal information base about group members. "Getting to know someone" via this medium is not as easily accomplished as it is in a face-to-face setting; and in a remote learning environment where individuals may be alone at their locations, it is probably even more important that some humanizing links be formed. In experimental studies, students noted that they "missed" not being able to *see* their teleconference instructor. It naturally follows that the studies showed that those instructors who made a number of personal visits to the distant classrooms, both before and during the course offerings (see "Clustering" in this chapter), noted that the students showed more positive feelings toward the mode of instruction.

Other ways of helping students identify with their instructor and other students include: providing a slide or picture of the teacher, sending a roster of participants to everyone in the class (this may include pictures of the class members also), and using names frequently when individuals make contributions to the discussion.

One of the simplest ways of humanizing is for the speaker to cultivate the use of naturalness and spontaneity of delivery. The telephone is considered to be a more intimate medium than radio and is conducive to an informal delivery style. A more relaxed and natural speaker will come across on the system more effectively.

Another key to successful humanizing is the use of a "local facilitator" who may be a community-based faculty member or a paraprofessional hired on a part-time basis. Local facilitators welcome participants at the beginning of the program; see that any materials needed for the meeting or class are available; and orient users new to the equipment by explaining how to participate. These on-site coordinators make sure that individuals feel at home in this environment.

Figure 2 suggests some of the humanizing techniques which might be used before, during, and after a teleconference. Descriptions of many of these techniques follow. "Hip pocket" techniques are those techniques which are easy to implement and allow an instructor to have some immediate successes with teleconferencing. Other, more involved techniques will be discussed following the "hip pocket" ideas. The quotations accompanying the text are taken from actual interviews with teleconference instructors.

"HIP POCKET" TECHNIQUES FOR HUMANIZING

- *Send a Welcome Letter*
  Let participants know they are important to the success of the program by sending them a welcome letter before the first teleconference. Include program goals, suggestions for preparing for the first session (such as a question or problem to think about), and some information about yourself (biographical sketch, photocopied picture).

- *Make a Master Roster*
  The more you know about the individuals in your group, the better you will communicate. Use information on preregistration lists to make up a master roster of participants at each location with a line or two of related information about them. Use this roster to focus discussion on the needs and interests of the individuals participating.

- *Use of Names*
  Always call participants by name. Use your roster list. When

---

Figure 2

Suggested Humanizing Techniques

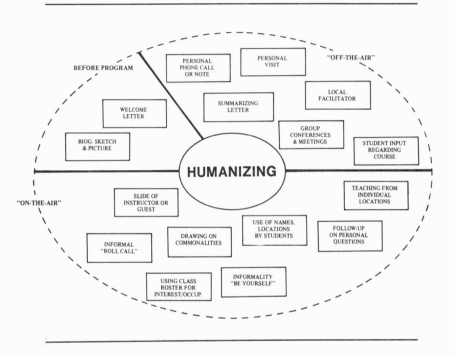

an individual asks a question, note the name, so you can use it again in your response. People like to be recognized by name; it is especially important in teleconferencing.

- *Let Your Personality Come Through*
  Be yourself. It is important to come across the way you do in a face-to-face situation, even though microphones are used for communicating. Try to form a mental picture of what it is like to be at one of the locations, and talk directly to individuals rather than to an "audience out there."

- *Open with an Informal "Roll Call"*
  To create an informal, friendly atmosphere and to give participants a chance to become accustomed to the equipment, ask for a few responses from selected locations. A few exchanges, such as "How's the weather?" or "How many are there with you today?," let individuals overcome hesitancy in using the microphones.

Set Up a Cluster Circuit

What is clustering? It is simply choosing one of the locations on the network as an origination point and asking all those participants within driving distance to meet with you there for that particular program in the series. One of the bonuses of teleconferencing is the capability of originating a program from any location on the network, and because we know that teleconferencing "works best" when individuals know something about one another, a strong recommendation exists to meet with groups at a local site.

Participants like it; programmers like it. Personal rapport is built, and it is an opportunity to gain feedback that could not be obtained in any other way. It is also a good chance to counsel with individuals who have specific concerns or who might just want to know you better—so if you are planning on using this technique, try to spend a couple of hours before or after your program to meet with group members.

How do you set up a cluster? Most programmers sit down

with a map of the area their program reaches. They pick out certain locations as the cluster sites—these are sites centrally located to the other locations. Many programmers set up an itinerary of the cluster locations which they plan to visit during the series. This "cluster circuit" may be announced during the first program or sent to participants in advance. Members have the option of attending the program at their own home bases or going to the session at the cluster site.

A nice addition to carry with you to the cluster location is a headset microphone, especially if you are used to working under hand-free studio conditions. It will allow you to focus your attention on your presentation and the group's interaction. What if you forget the microphone? A book placed on the top of a microphone press-bar will give you an "open line" during program time.

> *"The best thing is to try to get to locations within the first few weeks, if you can. I try to cluster every three, four, or five weeks. I run the broadcast from the location and will stay an extra two hours or so talking with individuals." (Education programmer.)*

Call on Commonalities

Individuals participating in teleconferences typically are diverse in background, education, and experiences. Goals may be diverse also. How can a programmer reach this broad range of individuals and generate a group feeling? Fortunately, we know from group dynamics theory that as individuals become aware of how their goals fit in with group goals, they become committed to the group—and rapport results.

To develop this awareness takes skill on the part of the programmer. One of the ways is to identify certain commonalities—shared experiences which can become the basis of a common goal or point of discussion among group members. The master roster is the best way to identify possible commonalities among participants. Several group members may have shared the same or similar experiences, even though they are at different locations. Ask these individuals to relate to the group their way of solving a particular problem—stress that even sharing a not-so-successful solution is "okay."

> *"Let's say we're talking about apprenticeship and I know from my roster that there are five or six people out there who work with an apprentice or have experience in this area. I'll ask them: 'What do you think about this—you're engaged in this activity.'"* *(Education programmer.)*

Local Facilitators

It is important in a distant learning system to provide students with some personal contact at the local level. Local facilitators may be students chosen from the group, paraprofessionals, or in the case of the large university extension networks—a university representative. For example, in every county courthouse, which is the central point in most small communities (like the town halls of New England), the Wisconsin system has an "LPA," a Local Program Administrator, who is responsible for all Extension programs in the community. The LPAs are likely to be professors of agronomy or resource development—they are the contemporary version of the "county agents" of former days. But whatever their specialties, they are full-fledged faculty members. And in addition to their substantive duties, their work also includes such tasks as registering walk-in students, insuring that recommended reading materials are stocked in the local library, and serving as the interface between the student and the institution—providing "humanizing" links on a one-to-one basis.

Other groups may use the network to provide training sessions for paraprofessionals or even professionals hired to perform the role of local facilitators. An example of this was the well-organized clergy program, which provided trained leaders to facilitate local groups in discussion of very personal issues. The success of this program was evidenced by the fact that support groups meeting on a regular basis grew out of the program series.

"Clergy don't feel comfortable discussing some issues on-the-air. That is why we chose to use the small-group method at each local site. We trained a highly qualified member of the group to perform the facilitator role at each site. These local faculty then used the telephone presentations as the theme or focus while discussion, case study, and role-playing provided vehicles for working on the issues." (*Clergy programmer.*)

Humanizing for Large Groups

With large audiences, it is just not possible to call everyone on a first-name basis or get to know individual interests, except in a very broad way. But don't forget the simple ways to humanize—the way you introduce a program by communicating your concern that each individual have a chance to have his or her needs met. Provide a mechanism for this: Give your phone number and phone-in office hours, or provide a postcard or prepaid mailer. Stress your interest in receiving these requests.

Even before the program, you can help individuals identify with you as an individual. Include a picture of yourself along with a short biographical sketch, either on the promotional brochure or in a short "welcome" letter.

As you are giving the program, think about the ways you can reach individuals. Use examples which relate to other areas the program reaches—not just local ones. Ask some participants from other locations to contribute to the program content.

When large numbers of people participate, time may run

out before all questions have been asked. An important part of humanizing is respecting the needs of individuals; thus, it is important to provide a vehicle that allows these participants to get answers to their questions. Provide this opportunity by having postcards available at locations or suggesting that you can be contacted during certain phone-in office hours the following day.

> *"I always provide some way—postcards perhaps—to allow for unanswered questions. I call it 'respect for my audience.' I know they came to the program because they had a question they wanted answered—and I want to be able to get that answer to them in some way." (Beekeeping programmer.)*

Humanizing When You Have Studio Participants

Many times, programmers ask the question, "Should I have a few participants in the studio with me for eye contact while I do my program?" This question has no one answer. Some programmers like to be alone in the studio—in this way, they can concentrate on all of the group members. They think that having a group with them tends to make them forget about the participants at other locations. Clearly, the decision must be made on the basis of the personal style of each instructor; however, if you do choose the on-site group option, a few do's may prove helpful.

- Remind your face-to-face group to use the microphones so that their comments and questions will go out over the network.
- Make sure your instructions and references are tailored to a teleconferencing setting—with more detailed directions being provided.
- Treat all comments and questions alike.

Humanizing Time—Establishing a Balance

Since humanizing techniques do take up "air time," a balance must be struck between making individuals feel comfortable with the system—generating rapport between you and other group members—and in presenting the program material. All programs will benefit from some portion of time spent in making individuals feel that they are an important part of the program.

However, the amount of getting-to-know-one-another and other humanizing will depend a great deal on the size of the group and the objectives of the teleconference. In a class on article-writing, for example, where group members' psychological support of one another's efforts is an important part of the growth process, humanizing time is well spent.

Participation in Teleconferencing

We want active participation in teleconferencing because we know it is important. Teleconferencing studies parallel those in other disciplines—educational psychology, communications, group dynamics. The chance to participate actively is central to the success of any learning or communication process.

Two guidelines might be noted in thinking about teleconference participation:

- Participation opportunities and strategies should be carefully planned in advance of program time.
- Participation involves not only encouraging group members to contribute to the program, but also the vital process of interacting with the content—what you are saying and the printed support materials.

Participation doesn't always "just happen" in teleconferencing. Studies suggest that there is an automatic training over time in which individuals consciously and unconsciously adapt their ways of communicating as they use an interactive system. However, some individuals adapt more quickly to a new situation; others may need added encouragement to do so. Building in participation formats as part of the program and asking some individuals to be responsible for taking the lead are ways to help assure that interaction will take place.

The second guideline concerns the fact that most of us think of participation as the kind in which we see an individual or group engaged in an activity of some sort: asking a question, making a comment, jotting down notes. The activity we see gives us confidence that the person is in the process of hearing and remembering what is being said.

However, the participation that we don't observe may be just as important in the communications process. Such things as active listening (anticipatory alertness) and mental work in thinking about a problem are important processes. Because we don't directly observe this participation, we tend to forget about it and its importance. By skillfully using questions, both written and oral, and by guiding group members in some mental exercises, you can stimulate this internal participation which is so critical in listening and learning.

Figure 3 shows some of the types of participation formats which might be used in a teleconference program. Many of these techniques have been freely adapted from adult education techniques to allow them to be used successfully in teleconferencing. "Hip pocket" techniques for participation as well as a number of the formats shown will be described in more detail on the following pages.

"HIP POCKET" TECHNIQUES FOR PARTICIPATION

* *Warm-Up Your Audience*
  Enthusiasm and encouragement by the programmer are vital to getting participation. Help individuals feel comfortable about sharing their experiences. Participants may need more encouragement than in a face-to-face setting, so your role as programmer is important.

Figure 3

Suggested Participation Techniques

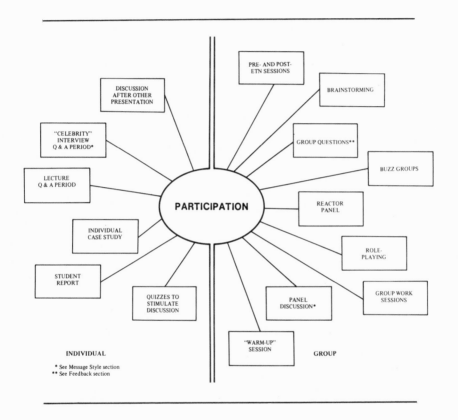

- *Plant Some Questions*

  Before the program, call a few specific participants and ask them to be ready with a comment or question, if the discussion should lag. You can use registration information to identify individuals who would be willing to assume this role. Such "planted" questions can help stimulate a chain reaction among group members.

- *Use Questions as a Tool*

  Use a list of highlight questions which summarize the main ideas for each session. Send these to participants before the program. Use this list to kick-off discussion by asking group members to pick out a question they would like to talk about in greater depth.

- *Use Interactive Formats*

  Use formats which encourage group members to participate. Almost all techniques used in adult education (case study, interview, panel discussion, role-playing) can be used successfully in teleconferencing. For example, a series of short case studies can be presented by individuals at the beginning of the program, with discussion following the case studies.

- *Get Specific Groups Involved*

  Ask a group at one of the locations to be responsible for the answer to a specific question to be presented at the next session. This responsibility encourages participants to sit down and talk with one another after program time. The technique also fosters cooperation—and there is a built-in lead-off for the next program's discussion.

Group-to-Group Discussion

This format gives participants at different locations a change of pace by giving them the chance to be the center of the discussion. It gives you, as the programmer, the opportunity to step back and monitor the participation. Get group-to-group discussion going by asking participants at one location to question participants at another location of their choice. You can do this spontaneously during program time, or you might assign the questioner role to a location during the prior session, so participants will be ready with questions. At program time, give that location the go-ahead and allow the participants to begin the discussion by calling on any location they wish to answer their questions.

"I try to plant seeds at the beginning—part of the reason we're together on a statewide network is to be able to share ideas and share experiences. As the series goes on, more and more people begin to feel comfortable in contributing." (Nursing programmer.)

Pre- and Post-Activities

These activities are useful in getting discussion going at locations. Is one of your goals to help individuals apply what they learned to their own situation? Use a post-activity. For example, after a program on burn care, a nursing clientele group might discuss the material presented during the program and apply it to their own hospital situation.

Sensitive issues which some groups might find difficult to discuss on-the-air may be handled as a pre- or post-activity. Clergy groups have successfully used this method to deal with a wide range of issues, meeting an hour before and an hour after the teleconference presentation. An example is the program on conflict management. Participants brought personal case studies. Local leaders (pastors and chaplains especially trained for this role) led the group discussion at the locations.

A less structured off-the-air activity may be generated by a programmer asking participants at a specific location to come up with the answer to an assigned question by the next program time.

"I like to get groups discussing among themselves at each of the sites. One way I do this is to ask that one group be ready to respond to a question the following week. I know that after we go off-the-air,

everyone will sit down and talk about what answer
they will give next time." (Education program-
mer.)

Group Work Session

This format is used to best advantage in demonstrating
manual skills and developing abilities by actually working on
a project under the direction of a teleconferencing programmer. Careful planning of these sessions is important so that
group leaders at locations can help individuals during the
session.

Packets with the necessary materials can be mailed directly
to individuals, or to a location, with some hard-to-mail items
being supplied by participants. Directions on how to proceed
are given over-the-air by the programmer, with local guidance
provided by on-location leaders.

"For my program on wood finishing, I send a
packet to every location containing everything
needed to learn about staining and finishing wood:
linseed oil, paint thinner, penetrating stain, mixing
tools, wood, even cloths to apply the stains and
finishes." (4-H programmer.)

Buzz Groups

Buzz groups at locations can be used off-the-air when the
topic to be discussed is best done in small groups. These small
groups, formed from a larger one, provide the most opportunity for everyone to participate.

Often called the six-six method, buzz groups usually
consist of six people who discuss a topic for six minutes
off-the-air at their locations. A later report-back is held on
the network. The six-six technique is useful following a panel
discussion or other presentation to draw out opinions of
group members.

In using buzz groups, use the following suggestions:

- Remember to keep the task simple: Develop one question, make two suggestions, agree on one disadvantage.
- Give specific time limits (minimum six minutes, maximum ten minutes).
- Make instructions clear and simple, using plenty of repetition.
- Have each group select a leader.
- State exactly what time groups will report back on the network.
- Have topics or questions for buzz groups typed and mailed in advance, if possible, so that each group has written instructions of the group's objectives.

Role-Playing

How do you make discussion more realistic? Get groups to thinking about how theory is translated into day-to-day behavior? Give adults a chance to try out new ways of acting in a "mistake-free" setting? Role-playing helps participants think about and practice human-relations skills under circumstances that approximate real life. Rather than just talking about something, role-playing is learning by doing-observing-analyzing.

How do you adapt role-playing to teleconferencing? The following ways have been successfully used by programmers.

(1) *Role-playing by group members; analysis by rest of group.* Preassign roles by calling several individuals before the program. Participants generally like to accept this responsibility—they say the anonymity of teleconferencing makes them feel more free to react realistically. Try to limit the number of voices to four at the maximum, so the audience can identify the individuals. (Give the members of the audience a chance to familiarize themselves with these voices by asking each role-player to give a short introduction of the role he or she will be playing before beginning.)

Prepare the group by suggesting things to watch for as the role-playing begins. Careful analyzing of what has happened is as important as the role-playing itself; analyzing helps the group pull out important issues involved.

(2) *Prerecorded vignettes of role-playing; analysis by group.* The second method of role-playing which works well in teleconferencing is to use prerecorded segments. These provide more control in terms of time and of issues brought out. This type of role-playing, although not "live," can still be as provocative and can lead to deep involvement in the issues by the audience in the analysis phase.

"We prerecorded four events that agency workers might run into in their day-to-day activities and taped them right on the scene so there were realistic background noises, etc. Each segment was about five minutes long and was followed up by an assignment for the next week. What would you have done in that situation?" (Social Work programmer.)

Reactor Panel

How do you "get the ball rolling" after a presentation? Use a reactor panel. It has been found in teleconferencing that participation by a few members of the group starts a chain reaction. The reactor panel is made up of a few members who take on the responsibility of reacting to a presentation.

Use the registration list to telephone two or three persons before the program and ask them to be ready to react. They can be at the same or different locations. Deciding on the reactor panel's objective will depend on the program:

• Will the panel be used to stimulate discussion by leading off with questions or thought-provoking ideas following a guest speaker?

• Will the panel serve as an audience representative to

interact with an outside speaker when the group is too large for individual questions?

Success depends in part on reactor panel members and the programmer agreeing on the objectives and procedures before the actual program.

"I would suggest calling people in advance and asking them to be responsible for reacting. You could say on-the-air, "Fond du Lac, Merrill, and Sheboygan—I want you as groups to serve as reactor panels." But that is not quite as successful. You will have some locations that will not reply. Having an individual *responsible works—he or she knows that he or she is* responsible *for a portion of the program." (Nursing programmer.)*

Brainstorming

Are you leading a meeting in which you need to generate a maximum number of ideas in a minimum of time? Adapt the brainstorming technique to teleconferencing.

Carefully set up the ground rules so that individuals know how to participate. After introducing the topic and procedures, use the open-mike technique, encouraging everyone to spontaneously participate.

You, as programmer, may need to manage the traffic flow. Be sensitive to attempts to enter the idea exchange. If large numbers of ideas come in at one time, you may have to ask for repeats. Allow silent periods for thinking and creativity, but start up the flow of ideas by reviewing some of those already given. Participants at locations may wish to make their own lists of ideas already given to use as a stimulus for further thinking; but, after the program, transcribe the ideas from the program tape and furnish a copy to each group member. Set aside a future program for the evaluation of the ideas presented.

Case Studies

Case studies can help group members uncover the problems and issues found in a particular situation being discussed. Case studies are detailed reports describing an event or a situation that a group can analyze and discuss. If you choose to use written case studies, a copy should be sent to each participant in advance of the program so that the cases can be read and digested.

An alternative which works well in a teleconference is to have individuals give oral case studies. Phone several participants before the program and ask them to present short case studies (five to ten minutes). As a programmer, you can help the group keep the details of the case in mind by summarizing the main points before opening up the discussion.

Since case studies tend to bring out strong opinions, they are a good way to generate participation by the group members.

"I consider the use of case studies as a 'pump-priming' activity. I wanted people to interact and we had a very diverse mixture of people—people who don't normally interact in their job situation. So why should I expect them to interact in a teleconference? I wanted that interaction—so I used case studies." (Social Work programmer.)

Participant Report

Just as in a face-to-face situation, you can assign individual participants a report or a project. The difference comes in how you use these reports in teleconferencing. You could have each individual give a short report on-the-air, letting others give feedback.

An individual might be assigned, for example, a five-minute report on how he or she is handling a current problem based on information given during a previous teleconference session.

"I've asked students to read a number of books or articles of their own choosing and then give a brief reaction on-the-air to the one they found most stimulating. The rest of the group then gave them feedback." (Education programmer.)

Question-and-Answer Periods

Don't overlook the question-and-answer period as a valuable way to get participation. You may have to adjust the way you handle these periods, depending on the size of the group. With small numbers (under 50), you can encourage group members to simply come on the network by identifying themselves and giving their questions.

With many locations represented, you may wish to ask certain geographic areas to respond at one time. Ask for questions from the northeast area, for example. If an individual group at one location has large numbers, questions may be written out, collected, and given to a group leader at that location.

Remember to have "respect" for questions that go unanswered because of lack of time (see Humanizing techniques). Provide some vehicle for getting answers to individuals.

"We are very protective about allowing enough time for the question-and-answer periods because we think they are so valuable. We feel that this is where a lot of the learning really takes place." (Medical programmer.)

Techniques for Handling "Silences" (Pauses) in Participation

One of the first things to remember is not to overreact to a silent period. One of the tendencies of a new programmer or guest speaker is to jump in too soon, without giving the audience time to respond. Not every moment of air-time needs to be filled—participants need time to phrase questions and develop answers.

Use a watch that has a second hand. Wait about 15 seconds before asking again for a response or going on with your presentation. Let your group know that you are allowing this time for responses.

If you would like to get further response and there is none, try these techniques:

- Rephrase your question. This may clarify any misunderstandings, and it gives a few more moments for participants to phrase an answer.
- Use directive techniques. Call on an individual from the roster (phrasing your question so that an individual has the option of not responding without losing face); or use a commonality of the group to stimulate a comment.
- Use a list of highlight questions. Run down the list and ask participants if they can answer all the questions based on the material presented during the program. If not, discuss one of the questions in further detail.

To summarize, it is important to remember that, in most cases, participation will take careful planning in a teleconferencing situation; that planning is done in advance of program time; and that participation is directive: people are asked to be responsible for initiating the participation.

Message Style in Teleconferencing

One important factor in designing purely aural messages is the difference between the rate at which we speak and the rate at which we think. The average rate of speech for most people is about 125 words per minute, while the brain processes data at much higher rates (one estimate is upwards of 300 words per minute). The ensuing gap often causes listeners' minds to wander. Instructors using teleconferencing (or in a face-to-face setting as well) should realistically acknowledge that much of their listening group will be distracted at any given moment. Repetition and summary can help provide cues for those listeners whose thoughts have momentarily strayed.

Fatigue which results from listening to an aural message over an extended period of time is another factor to consider. Listening research indicates that this tired feeling is the result of restlessness and boredom. It is suggested that messages be designed to incorporate more variety, such as using shorter modules and greater change of pace. One study of classroom instruction via teleconferencing found that students preferred lecture segments of not more than 25 minutes in length. Longer teleconferences can include a variety of activities, not just "straight" lectures. Programs running more than 50 minutes in length should provide a "break" so that both students and instructors can continue with the succeeding segments more relaxed and refreshed.

When we listen to a speaker, verbal cues can help emphasize the important ideas that the speaker wants to be remembered. The use of phrases such as, "Now, remember this," or "This is important," and paragraphs which introduce the message content appear to improve the reception and retention of the material. Overviews ("advance organizers") of the concept to be covered have been demonstrated to be of value in guiding the students to the succeeding materials.

Printed support materials, such as outlines, word lists, supplementary articles, bibliographies, and graphics (charts, tables, and drawings) help support the audio message by providing a second channel for the information. Print also serves as a permanent record and reviewing device.

In general, the more "interesting" a speaker can make his or her message, the more attentive each individual will be and the more will be remembered. Speakers who can use illustrations and examples that relate to the frames of reference of the listening group and who punctuate their message with vivid detail, which individuals can use to develop clear, mental images of the content, will be able to keep interest levels high as well as increase the chances that the information will be retained by their listeners.

Figure 4 shows a few of the techniques relevant to message style. Following are a few "hip pocket" techniques as well as other message formats. A special look at the lecture focuses on one of the most commonly used presentation styles.

"HIP POCKET" TECHNIQUES FOR MESSAGE STYLE

• *Preview Your Message*
Give a preview of what you are going to say in the form of a short, general overview. Giving individuals an idea in advance of the various parts of a message and how it will be organized (from general ideas to specific examples, or vice versa) helps them in their own understanding and remembering processes.

• *Use Variety*
Plan for short segments. Variety keeps interest levels high and this leads to more active listening. Keep your program fast-paced, providing short segments of concentrated listening (10-15 minutes) alternated with other activities. These activities might range from a simple question-and-answer period to the use of a buzz group (adaptation of the six-minute-six-people discussion technique) at each location.

• *Repeat and Summarize Main Points*
Use repetition and summary to help individuals remember important points. Repeat new words, concepts, or phrases at least three times during an hour program. New words can be spelled on-the-air to aid audience understanding, or a printed word list can be added to the packet of materials sent to individuals.

• *Provide Print Backup*
Use print materials to back up your message—an outline, some illustrative brochures, or even a detailed workbook. Print rein-

Figure 4

Suggested Message Style Techniques

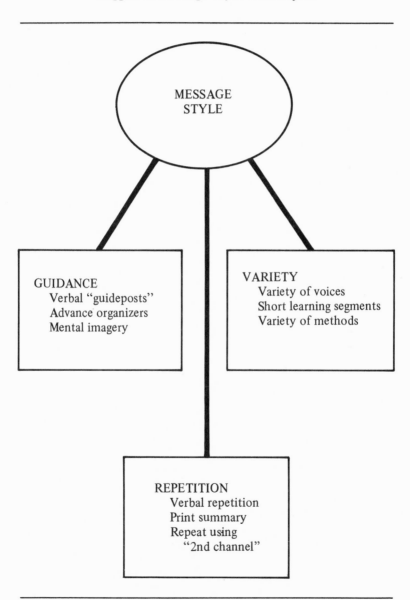

forces what we hear and is a permanent record for review purposes.

• *Send a Summary Letter*
The most important summary is at the end of the program. If time runs out, a short summary letter could be used to tie together some of the important points brought out during a panel discussion or interview.

Lecture

One of the formats you will probably choose most often is the lecture, which is popular because it is an efficient way of presenting factual information. But it can also be, whether face-to-face or via teleconferencing, a very uninteresting way to get information. Dynamic, interesting presentations are the goal of any speaker. However, one of the tendencies for lecturers over a teleconferencing system is to begin the program enthusiastically, then eventually trail off sentences or begin to speak in monotone. To overcome these tendencies and to create more effective lectures, try some of the techniques below.

How to Maintain Your Enthusiasm in Lectures

• "Interrupt" yourself to change your pitch and volume. Use reminders to do this, for example, on your outline or written script, leave out certain figures or dates or circle some items in red as a signal to yourself to change your voice level and inflection.
• Speak to individuals, not to an audience. Mentally picture participants at each location. Speak to them as individuals, not as a group.
• Encourage feedback to generate your own enthusiasm for what you are saying. Mark spots on your outline where you feel a natural question might arise in the minds of your listeners.
• Do use a lead-up to the question. Saying "Any questions?" generally won't bring a response. Provide a natural progression, a jumping-off point for the question.

How to Maintain Participant Enthusiasm
- Stimulate individuals to interact with what you are presenting. Use questions for this. Ask them to anticipate:
  "What factors do you think were responsible for this situation?"
  Ask them to compare and contrast:
  "As I am presenting this next section, think about whether what I am saying makes sense in light of what you already know."
- Get individuals to interact with the print materials you have mailed out. Color code or number sections to make it easier for individuals to locate materials during the program. Ask them to look at a chart, read a list of considerations, or react to a statement in an article.
- Vary the pacing of the program. Use faster pacing when reviewing, slower pacing when covering new material.
- Use shorter periods of lecturing intermixed with group feedback. A 12- to 15-minute period is ideal; 20 to 25 minutes is the maximum for continuous speaking by one individual.
- Be realistic about the amount of material to be covered. A good rule-of-thumb is to present three major ideas in a 30-minute period. Use plenty of amplifying examples.
- Use mental imagery as much as possible. Use examples which help participants picture the point you are trying to make.
- Combine your lecture with other techniques. Use a prerecorded vignette or interview; have a guest present part of the material; plan a participant report; call on a panel.
- Above all, relax and enjoy yourself. If you are having fun and are enthusiastic about what you are saying, your group members will be enthusiastic as well.

Panel Discussion

A good alternative to presenting the information yourself is to use a panel discussion composed of resource people. This format is especially good in situations where complex or controversial issues are being explored. The advantage in teleconferencing is that not all the panel members need to be with you at the program origination point. They can be brought into the network from various points—home, office (or even, as in a very unusual case—from an airport phone booth).

Panels, simply because they might present diverse opinions, need the guiding hand of the programmer to help focus the discussion, bring out important points, and provide an overall summary. Here are some "do's" that may prove helpful:

- Limit a panel to four people for voice recognition by the audience.
- Phone prospective members in advance to test out how well they might come across in a teleconferencing mode.
- Provide panel members with advance information about the audience they will be talking with and a few techniques for using teleconferencing.
- Provide participants with some material to read or some questions to think about before the teleconference so that the panel doesn't come on "cold."
- Provide a final summary, either at the end of the program or via a summary letter.

"Panel members don't have to be with you at the program origination point—we patched panel members in from different locations. In fact, one was home eating his lunch, one was in her office, and another attended the teleconference with other participants at one of the locations." (Social Work programmer.)

Interview

Another way to vary your presentation is to use an interview format. The interview is ideal for teleconferencing. It adds informality and spontaneity and helps to keep the pace of the program moving. Not only is the interview an excellent audio technique, but, like the panel discussion, it allows the programmer to bring in resource people who might otherwise not be available to the group.

Conducting an interview is quite easy and inexpensive. For

example, a phone call to the guest could be made to his or her office or home. Audience members would be invited to interact with this resource person after you begin the interview. Or, as an option, a short, prerecorded presentation by your guest could be used to kick-off a question-and-answer period during which the guest would be "on-line" for discussion with the group. Some suggestions for conducting interviews:

- Remind the person being interviewed that short, concise answers are best. Many times, persons inexperienced in using teleconferencing make their replies more lengthy than they ordinarily would face-to-face. You can help to keep the interview moving and to the point.

- As for a panel discussion, prepare the guest with some background material about your audience, main objectives of the interview, perhaps even a course outline. A sample cassette of a previous program is helpful to guests.

- Prepare your audience to interact with the speaker. Warm them up before the interview by introducing the topic to be discussed. Give them background information about the guest. Ask them to prepare questions in advance.

- Help to make the interview meaningful by making frequent summaries, transitions, clarifying points, and tying the presentation together.

"An interview of 20 minutes plugged into a program can be very meaningful. I ask participants to send me a list of questions they would like to have me ask. I use perhaps six or eight selected questions that seem to be very important, with the guest live and on-line. Then we just open up the network so that the participants can talk with the resource person." (Education programmer.)

A Special Kind of Interview—Celebrity Expertise

One of the most successful ways of introducing individuals to teleconferencing is to give them the opportunity to "meet" celebrities in a specialty field. Because teleconferencing can reach these celebrities without travel on their part, opportunities to include them in programs have been widened. People known nationally and internationally in the fields of medicine, theology, music, and photography, to list just a few examples, have been part of teleconferences.

To assure the success of this special kind of interview, planning is important. Follow the guidelines suggested for the interview format. In addition, remember that although gifted individuals may feel comfortable in their own creative activity, they may not be as comfortable in describing their skill or in teaching it to a group. One programmer opens the program with his guest by discussing a common interest, thereby putting the guest at ease before moving on to his or her presentation.

> *"By going to artists wherever they are via teleconferencing, they can be persuaded to participate in an adult education venture like this—they don't have to lose travel time." (Music programmer.)*

Using Other Media Channels to Support Your Message

Print as a Complement. It is not surprising that the perfect complement to a teleconference is some type of printed material. Outlines, word lists, supplementary articles, bibliographies, and graphics (charts, tables, and drawings) not only help support the audio message but also serve as a permanent record and reviewing device. Print eliminates time spent note-taking—time which might be more profitably devoted to listening and thinking.

Topic Outlines. A topic outline, as used in teleconferencing, is similar to the outlines used by many speakers (a skeleton profile of the material to be presented) with two exceptions: (1) plenty of white space in which to take notes, and (2) a very detailed numbering system. For example, in section three of the outline you might find under the major heading of "3.00," the minor points, "3.01," "3.02," etc. You, as a speaker, refer to these points as you go along. If a question is raised, an individual can easily say, "Back under point #2.01, would you please explain further?"

Summary Letters for Spontaneous Programming. If your programs consist mainly of spontaneous programming—panel discussion, interview, etc.—in which you don't always know in advance what points will be made, you can still use print backup. After the program, pick out the main points brought out in a panel discussion or interview and jot them down in the form of a personal letter to your group members. Your approach might be: *"Here are some of the things I got out of last week's session."* These letters can be inexpensively duplicated and then personally signed by you.

Slides and Other Visuals. In the early uses of teleconferencing, slides were thought to be essential to the program—as a program focus for students. Obviously, there are some disciplines in which the use of slides is critical in understanding the content. For example, in programs on art, photography, and medicine, a color presentation of visual material may be central to the learning process.

However, with the skilled use of print materials, experience now indicates that slides or overhead graphics are not really essential or even necessary to most programs. A good idea is to incorporate necessary graphics into the printed materials by using inexpensive photocopying services. (Note: Remember to check copyright guidelines when reproducing printed materials.)

Feedback in Teleconferencing

The last component in the Teletechniques instructional design model is feedback. Theorists tell us that feedback is an essential ingredient in the communications process. So central is this "return loop" to any person-to-person exchange that it is seldom consciously thought about. For example, when we interact with a group in a face-to-face setting, subtle feedback in the form of non-verbal cues is constantly helping us gain information about how the message is being received. Yawns or bored expressions are forms of "negative" feedback which stimulate us to change what we are saying or how we are saying it; erect postures and looks of interest are forms of positive feedback which reinforce and provide motivation for future communication.

This non-verbal feedback is not present in teleconferencing. Fortunately, we can plan ahead to provide mechanisms for kinds of feedback other than non-verbal. Thus, feedback as a design component in teleconferencing centers around those mechanisms or techniques which will complete the communications loop between you and the participants.

The easiest way to incorporate feedback in a teleconference is to plan for verbal feedback from the group. After each natural division in the material, you can ask questions: Was the message too fast? Too complex? Clearly explained? Planning for this type of structured feedback is generally the most successful in a teleconference, but there are alternatives. You could use a less structured type by suggesting that members of the group interrupt at any time. If you use this approach, remember to be sensitive to attempts by group members to interrupt. You may also wish to assign the feedback role to a number of members of the group in advance of program time (see *Reactor Panel* in Participation section of this chapter). Your choice depends a great deal on your delivery style, the content, and the type of group participating.

Feedback's importance to you and the individuals participating cannot be overemphasized. Whether the teleconference's objective is to provide education to a group of students or centers around decision-making in an administrative meeting, people want and need to know "how they are doing." Providing both verbal and written channels to communicate this information to them is invaluable, not only for corrective action but also for motivation.

Self-feedback can be an excellent tool to improve next week's or next year's program. Many instructors use the previous program tape to do some self-diagnosing. What were the strengths and weaknesses of that program? What might be changed in time for the next session? Were opportunities provided for participation? Did individuals take advantage of those opportunities? Did the message come across with enthusiasm—naturalness? This type of self-feedback can be as important as that which we get from program participants.

Figure 5 presents a number of ways to obtain feedback on the ongoing program, overall program, and student progress. Some "hip pocket" techniques follow as well as types of written feedback devices and a more formal evaluation system.

"HIP POCKET" TECHNIQUES FOR FEEDBACK

- *Ask for Feedback*
  The most basic technique for getting feedback is simply to ask for it during the program. Check on your pacing and on the quality of the reception at the locations. Ask the group if there are questions about the material you are discussing. Because individuals new to teleconferencing may be shy about giving feedback, preassign it, calling several people in advance of the program.

- *Use On-the-Spot Application of Information*
  Find out if the material being presented is relevant to participants' situations. Pause several times during the presentation to ask for individual feedback. Ask one or two participants to briefly comment on the value of the information to him or her (or them). Would the person use it? If so, how? Application-of-information feedback stimulates others to think creatively.

Figure 5

Suggested Feedback Techniques

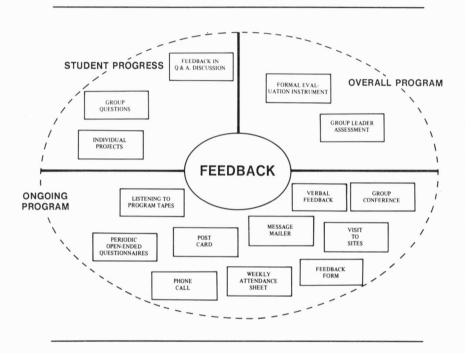

- *Use Group Questions*
  Instead of evaluating participants individually, use a weekly question which is discussed and answered after program time by groups at locations. A group working to develop a cooperative best answer stimulates rapport and helps give individuals more in-depth understanding. Have group members sign their names to the answer (allowing for a minority opinion) and mail it to you for evaluation before the next program.

- *Use Written Forms of Feedback*
  Use written methods to determine whether your program is meeting its objectives. A postcard questionnaire or a preaddressed mailer with space for comments can be included with print materials sent out before the program.

- *Listen to Tapes*
  Teleconferences tend to be concentrated periods of listening and interaction. Many times, programmers miss an important ingredient in the program because there just wasn't time to stand back and be an observer. Listening to the recorded program can be a valuable feedback tool.

Verbal Feedback

Give verbal acknowledgment whenever a comment is made by a group member, and ask all participants to do the same. For example, a simple, "Yes, I see," or "Fine" (or whatever phrase is appropriate), is feedback in its most simple form, but it is important because it tells the participants that the message was received. In the absence of non-verbal cues, such as the nod of your head, these short phrases help to guide the flow of the communications process. Correspondingly, remind yourself that when you give a response to a question not to "overtalk." As we are explaining a point, we may give too much information because we are not sure if the individual received our message. Ask for verbal feedback. Give a basic explanation, pause, ask, "Does this answer your question, or shall I go on?"

Question-and-Answer Periods

Question-and-answer periods have been described in the section on Participation. Another mention is warranted here because this is one of the times during a program in which you get valuable feedback information from your group members about how well the message is coming across. Also, these periods provide an opportunity for you to get immediate, corrective feedback to individuals.

Rather than thinking of this type of format as a question-and-answer *period*, it might be better to integrate it into the program. Feedback can be going on during the entire presentation, rather than only during a formalized time period. By asking for an occasional question (or asking one yourself) as you go along, you break up the listening, stimulate thinking, and motivate yourself by getting an audience feedback.

"You need to break in, I find, rather frequently. Perhaps every ten minutes, maybe just using a Socratic thing of question-and-answer. The presentations have to be held to briefer lengths than what you'd use for a campus class where you have face-to-face contact." (Education programmer.)

Feedback Form

Use a "feedback form" that asks for very basic information and can be filled out in about five minutes by the participants. Questions might be as shown in Figure 6.

Formal Feedback in a Meeting (Voting Procedures)

With many of the teleconferencing systems available, the technology will allow for a voice vote. Simply asking everyone who votes aye (or nay) to press and speak into his or her mike will work well if the vote is not a close decision.

A mail-in vote can be facilitated by using a simple, standard rating-scale form which can be used in a variety of

Figure 6

Feedback Form

---

1. What is your overall reaction to this session? Circle one number.

   1   2   3   4   5   6   7   8   9   10

   extremely   extremely
   unfavorable   favorable

2. What do you think were the strengths and weaknesses in this session?

3. How would you suggest the next session be improved?

4. Other comments, suggestions.

---

ways (see Figure 7). For example, a simple yes or no vote on any issue can be obtained by the chairperson asking individuals to check the "1" column if the vote is yes and the "2" column if the vote is no.

If a more quantified rating about a particular issue is desired, participants could use the "1" through "5" columns to vote on a particular issue. For example, in voting on the advisability of adopting an administrative guideline, participants might register their opinions by checking the appropriate columns:

1—extremely unfavorable;

2—unfavorable;

3—neutral;

4—favorable; and

5—extremely favorable.

Figure 7

A Standard Rating Scale Form

```
+----------------------------------------------------------+
|                                                          |
|            MULTIPURPOSE RATING SCALES                    |
|                                                          |
|          1        2        3        4        5           |
|     A.   □        □        □        □        □           |
|                                                          |
|          1        2        3        4        5           |
|     B.   □        □        □        □        □           |
|                                                          |
|          1        2        3        4        5           |
|     C.   □        □        □        □        □           |
|                                                          |
|          1        2        3        4        5           |
|     D.   □        □        □        □        □           |
|                                                          |
|          1        2        3        4        5           |
|     E.   □        □        □        □        □           |
|                                                          |
|          1        2        3        4        5           |
|     F.   □        □        □        □        □           |
|                                                          |
|          1        2        3        4        5           |
|     G.   □        □        □        □        □           |
|                                                          |
+----------------------------------------------------------+
```

Message Mailers

The message mailer encourages participants to communicate their feedback to you. By providing this form as a part of a set of printed materials, you are conveying the unspoken message that you are sincerely interested in obtaining feedback from the individuals in your group.

A message mailer can be very simply designed. It can be of any size and shape. (Note: You may wish to check current postal guidelines for size regulations.) Its basic ingredients are:

- provision for comments and questions;
- space for name and address of participant;
- preaddressed to you; and
- postage prepaid (optional).

The message mailer's exact form is open to creativity. It might be called by a title, such as, "OPEN LINE." It can be color-coded so that each mailer corresponds to a section in the print materials dealing with a particular topic. If you have a series of five programs, you can easily identify a yellow form returned to you, for example, as dealing with a particular program in the series.

Formal Evaluation Instrument

After planning and implementing a teleconference, it is important to gather information on how well the program objectives were met. Because teleconferencing is a unique medium for instruction and communications, any evaluation device should be specifically designed to measure the interrelationships of many factors.

The primary aspects of a teleconference are:

- lecturer's behavior— the way the message is delivered by the programmer or guest speaker;
- program aide's behavior— the performance of the persons who serve as facilitators at the remote locations;
- environment— the arrangement of physical facilities, seating, lighting, etc., at remote locations;
- technical components— the functioning of the technology;
- program materials— the use of support materials including audio-visuals and printed materials;

- program process—   the involvement of the par-
                       ticipants in the presentation
                       and discussion of the pro-
                       gram content; and
- program influence—   the impact of the program
                       on the participants.

Statements are developed which examine various characteristics of each factor. Generally, at least five items are used
for each aspect of the teleconference (such as technical
quality) in order to gain a good "reading" on that subgroup.
Sample statements under technical quality might be:

- "The reception at my location was satisfactory."
- "The programmer's voice was clear and distinct as it
  came over the network."
- "The teleconferencing equipment was easy to operate."

The final instrument will be about three dozen items in
length, with statements about the content, lecturer, materials, organization, physical facilities, and the technical quality.
These statements are then rated on a numerical scale by
program participants to determine how closely the statement
matches the actual teleconferencing experience.

You may also wish to include questions regarding demographic information on participants, such as educational
background, professional experience, present occupational
position, major areas of responsibility, motivation for atten-
dance, age, and sex. The demographic section gives you an
"audience profile" which assists in interpreting the data.

Evaluation results are primarily used to judge program
effectiveness. But some side benefits occur. One is that
the very process of analyzing the evaluation may stimulate
the reshaping of some of your overall goals and values in the
educational/communications process. The evaluation process
also provides one more channel of communication between
you and the participants. It is a concrete sign that you are

interested in what the individuals have to say about a program.

Summary

To summarize the use of the Teletechniques model, four simple steps are used to present techniques which are used in designing an effective, satisfying teleconference—humanizing, participation, message style, and feedback. Since the use of teleconferencing cuts across subject matter areas, length of program times, types of student groups, sizes of audiences, and numbers of programs within a given course, not all of the suggested techniques are directly applicable to an individual program. However, they may stimulate other approaches on the part of the individual programmer.

In order to see how the Teletechniques model might be used in a typical program, Figure 8 presents a one-hour teleconference session which incorporates some of the techniques (techniques are in bold face).

References

Beavers, A.W. A Case Study of Organizing for a Telelecture Course. *The Status of the Telephone in Education,* University of Wisconsin-Extension, Madison, May 1976.

Burkhart, J.A. An Experiment to Determine the Values of Using Amplified Telephone Interviews. Stephens College, Columbia, Missouri, 1969.

Casey, A.E., and M.C. Havron. Human Needs in Teleconferencing. *A/V Communications,* April 1974.

Glueck, W.F. Management Training Using Telelecture. *Training and Development Journal,* November 1971.

Hoyt, D.P., and D.W.M. Frye. *The Effectiveness of Telecommunication as an Educational Delivery System.* Final Report for National Center for Educational Research and

Development, Kansas State University, Manhattan, Kansas, June 1972.

Jesser, D.L., and M.J. Clarke. *Art by Telephone.* Carson City, Nevada: Western States Small Schools Project, 1966.

Kreitlow, B.W. Tuskegee, Are You on the Line? *Adult Leadership,* November 1974.

Monson, M. A Report Investigating Teaching Techniques Used Over the Educational Telephone Network. In *A Design for Interactive Audio,* University of Wisconsin-Extension, Madison, 1977.

Parker, L.A., and M. Baird. Humanizing Telephone-Based Instructional Programs. University of Wisconsin-Extension, Madison, 1975.

Sampson, H.E. Credit Course Instruction Via ETN: A Case Study. *The Telephone in Education—Book II,* University of Wisconsin-Extension, 1977.

Short, J. Teaching by Telephone—The Problems of Teaching Without the Visual Channel. *Teaching at a Distance,* November 1974. No. 1.

Sparks, J. Helping Clergy Use Conflict Creatively. *Adult Leadership,* February 1976.

Williams, E. A Review of Psychological Research Comparing Communications Media. *The Status of the Telephone in Education,* University of Wisconsin-Extension, Madison, 1976.

Figure 8

A Sample Teleconference Session

OPTIMUM PROGRAM CONDITIONS:
A packet of materials sent prior to program to each participant containing: **topic outline** or agenda, list of highlight questions, selected reading material, biographical sketch and picture of speaker/instructor, and **welcome letter.** A local facilitator at each site to provide physical facilities conducive to teleconferencing, to welcome participants, and to demonstrate how to use equipment.

20 min. PREPROGRAM ACTIVITY (optional)
> Activity done by local group to warm-up for program: discussion, problem-solving, group work, or arriving at a cooperative answer to problem assigned the week before.

10 min.* PREVIEW
> (*initial session of ongoing series)
> To humanize and elicit participation, open the program by introducing yourself and any speakers. Welcome your audience and emphasize the ease of use of equipment and encourage participation by asking for an **informal roll call,** selecting a few individuals to come on the network.
> Ask participants to fill out a 5 x 7 card with personal information that can be compiled into a **master roster** list by location.
> Stress that you are trying to meet all individuals' needs. Give a phone number they can call or suggest dropping a postcard in the mail if there is an unanswered question.
> Review course objectives/meeting goals and how they may be reached.
> Give an **advance organizer** in the form of a general overview of material to be presented.

> (*2nd program of ongoing series)
> Use this time to review the material covered in the last session, answer any questions from the group, and introduce new topic via **advance organizer.**

(Continued on Next Page)

Figure 8 (Continued)

40 min. PRESENT

Divide these 40 minutes into shorter segments providing time for feedback, question-and-answer, or discussion. Rule-of-thumb: three major ideas presented every 30 minutes.

For example: 10 min. Presentation of new material via topic outline.

5 min. Participant feedback via Q & A. (Use some **planted questions.**)

10 min. Interview: prerecorded or "live" with resource person.

10 min. Participant **reactor panel** in exchange with resource person.

5 min. Feedback application: one or two participants suggest application.

10 min. REVIEW

Summary: important points brought out and summarized. Highlight questions used as a basis to clear up any misunderstandings and to stimulate thinking for next session.

Groups at local site may be given a question to answer on a cooperative basis to kick-off discussion for next program.

20 min. POSTPROGRAM ACTIVITY (optional)

Group discussion of application of material to their own situation or **group questioning.**

IV.

OUTCOMES

Increasing the effectiveness of individual teleconferences has been the focus of this book. The Teletechniques model presents guidelines which enable an instructor or moderator to design more *effective* instructional sessions as well as more *satisfying* ones. But these techniques are but a smaller part of the larger picture concerning the *overall effectiveness* of teleconferencing. This chapter presents a look at what we know in answer to the questions: Is teleconferencing effective? What are the benefits of using teleconferencing for students, teachers, educational administrators, and educational institutions?

Research in teleconferencing is ongoing. The field is new—only a little over a decade old as of 1980. But in these years, we have documentation from both ends of the spectrum: research done under laboratory conditions as well as in day-to-day applications in the field. Although the studies are uncoordinated—using a number of different designs—and although many of the experiments were conducted prior to the advent of adequate technical teleconferencing equipment, a review of the literature shows success. Studies across various content areas have measured the cognitive gains of classes taught via teleconferencing. In all cases, teleconferencing was as effective as face-to-face instruction.

A few research studies are summarized below:

- *Mathematics.* Telelecture was used for retraining elementary school mathematics teachers. Pretests and posttests of achievement, mathematical ability, and attitude inventory were given to individuals taught in a conventional face-to-face setting and via telelecture. There was a significantly greater mean change in content mastery for the telelecture group than for the conventionally taught group.
- *Hebrew.* Studies of adult classes in reading and writing Hebrew were made. The classes were taught simultaneously to two groups in Michigan via teleconferencing and to a control group in Chicago. Scores on a midterm and on an oral reading test indicated no significant difference between performance of the three groups.
- *Money Management.* Evaluations were made of county extension homemakers' groups in Kansas. The groups were enrolled in a short course on money management. Pretests and posttests given to those taught by traditional face-to-face lecture and those instructed by telephone showed no significant differences.
- *Psychology.* Three classes in introductory psychology at the University of Missouri-St. Louis were compared, using telelecture and on-campus instruction. Tests of all three groups showed no difference.
- *Mining, Engineering, Modern Mathematics.* College classes at West Virginia University, Morgantown, were compared with extension classes taught via telelecture and electrowriter in mining, engineering, and modern mathematics. The analysis of the groups showed that achievement by extension classes taught via teleconferencing was equal to or significantly greater than that of students in the on-campus classes.

More research needs to be done. Additional questions–beyond the traditional ones asked by comparison studies of teleconferencing vs. face-to-face instruction which focus mainly on cognitive gain–need to be asked. What is the best mix of teleconferencing and supporting visuals; of network and audience size? What about the use of professional talent? These and many other questions are raised by looking at the data from case studies of successful teleconferencing courses. The data merely open up new avenues of inquiry. For example, "inactive nurses" enrolled in refresher courses that were taught via teleconferencing were surveyed. Results indicated that 12 percent of the nurses actually returned to work and a smaller percent said they planned on returning sooner than they had anticipated. The question then arises: What role did the teleconferencing course play in their decision to return to work?

We have briefly sketched a picture of what we know about teleconferencing. These studies, as well as many informal descriptive accounts, in addition to the experience we have had in developing, implementing, and evaluating a large network for over 13 years, form the basis for an aggregate list of the uses and benefits of teleconferencing. The following benefits, grouped according to students, teachers, educational administrators, and educational institutions, suggest the functions that teleconferencing can perform effectively in an educational context.

Basic Benefits of Using Teleconferencing

1. *Effectiveness.* Research indicates that it is a highly effective delivery technique in communicating educational materials to students throughout a large geographical area.

2. *Economy.* It is frequently less expensive per student contact hour when compared to other instructional media.*

*The cost of the Wisconsin-Extension ETN system averages 25 cents per student contact hour.

It requires no large capital outlay to get started and no large, long-range dollar commitments to operate.

3. *Simplicity.* The technology is relatively simple and easily understood and operated. The telephone is a familiar instrument that most people are comfortable with—and teleconferencing station equipment is just one step beyond this type of technology.

4. *Interactive Capability.* Unlike other media, the telephone is a talk-back medium with immediate two-way interaction. Television, radio, film, and audio-cassettes—in fact, most of educational technology in general—do not have this interactive feature, this built-in feedback capability.

5. *Easy-Access Technology.* Telephones are everywhere and they can be easily accessed for educational purposes. There is no need for special buildings, setups, locations, or prescheduling—the telephone is there and ready to use at a moment's notice.

6. *Here-and-Now Technology.* The telephone is here-and-now technology. It is operational; it has the "bugs" worked out; procedures have already been developed to maintain it.

7. *Flexible in Time-Space Frames.* The telephone is literally available any time of the day or night, every day of the week. The station equipment can be moved to anywhere there is a telephone connection—no matter how large or small the room—and the meeting facility needs no special requirements such as acoustical treatment, etc.

8. *Intimacy.* The medium "demands" participation by the listener. There is a sense of involvement and intimacy felt on the part of the group members.

9. *Specialization.* It is good for reaching very large audiences or very small ones. It can serve the specialized interests of very small clusters of people in any single place, making it possible to reach isolated professionals who might otherwise be in an educational vacuum; working people, students in isolated schools, homebound or hospitalized

students. It facilitates the reaching of new audiences ordinarily neglected.

10. *Immediacy.* It makes available front-line information from distantly located top authorities. It provides truly continuing education in that it lends itself to transmitting *limited* amounts of information *frequently* (allowing for assimilation of new information into the daily activities of learners) instead of *mass* doses of information *infrequently.*

Now, more specifically, let us explore how these qualities of teleconferencing relate to the students', instructors', and educational administrators' frame of reference, as well as to the overall needs of the educational institutions.

Advantages for Students

1. Teleconferencing can meet the needs of students in remote locations. Some professionals have indicated they would not have settled in smaller communities,* if continuing education via a teleconferencing system had not been available.

2. Through teleconferencing, students can take advantage of quality education at reasonable costs. They are not required to travel great distances or spend large amounts of time away from family or occupational responsibilities.

3. Students learn as much or more in teleconferences as in other modes of learning.

4. Outstanding teachers are available across broad geographical areas that might not be accessible to students in any other way.

5. Teleconferencing allows personalized communication between student and instructor as well as between students at a variety of locations.

*Refers to Wisconsin survey opinion.

Advantages for Instructors

1. Teleconferencing allows a sharing of faculty resources, enabling schools to offer more complete educational programs. For example, in a community college system, a professor taught a small class in engineering mechanics (statics) each semester. Other campuses in the system could not afford to offer statics as part of their curriculum. Through teleconferencing, the instructor now offers the course to all 14 campuses.

2. There is great economy in both time and money. Faculty are not required to travel great distances or spend large amounts of time away from their primary teaching responsibilities.

3. There is flexibility in program planning and scheduling. Systems can accommodate prerecorded tape materials as well as live lectures.

4. Programs can originate from any location on the network, allowing instructors to give a program from a location which might be more convenient during a trip or conference away from home.

Advantages for Educational Administrators

1. Teleconferencing systems may be used for administrative purposes when not set aside for instructional purposes.

2. Teleconferencing systems can be integrated into other types of instructional systems, such as multimedia systems, computer-assisted instruction, and programmed instructional systems.

3. Teleconferencing has a primary advantage over most other instructional media in that it permits two-way interaction between instructor and students and among students.

4. The public relations aspects are significant. The programs presented via teleconferencing are tangible evidence that an institution is vitally concerned with the day-to-day problems of professionals and consumers, as opposed to the

more esoteric research which slowly filters down to the local level.

Advantages for Educational Institutions

1. Teleconferencing enables institutions to reach entirely new audiences which have previously been neglected. In one state, a hospital program was offered to more than 400 housekeepers and 300 food service workers. Prior to this offering, there were few continuing education programs for these personnel. Even if courses were available, it was difficult to gain release time and travel expense money for these individuals to attend classes outside of the hospital location.

2. Teleconferencing enables an institution to respond quickly and efficiently to the specialized educational needs of groups scattered throughout geographical areas.

3. Institutions can offer classes simultaneously to a limited number of locations. It allows sharing of costs and of faculty resources.

4. Teleconferencing is frequently less expensive per student contact hour than other mediated instruction.

5. Teleconferencing can increase enrollments.

6. Teleconferencing can serve the needs of society by bringing quality education to rural areas with sparse populations and to the underprivileged in cities.

References

Beattie, T., and P. Frick. *The Telephone Method of Teaching.* Colorado Department of Education, Denver, 1963. ERIC ED 036-357.

Becker, A.D. Teleconferencing—A Survey and Evaluation. *Journal of Communication,* Summer 1978.

Blackwood, H., and C. Trent. *A Comparison of the Effective-*

ness of Face-to-Face and Remote Teaching in Communicating Educational Information to Adults. Kansas State University, Manhattan, School of Education, June 1972.

Boswell, J.J., D.W. Mocker, and W.C. Hamlin. Telelecture: An Experiment in Remote Teaching. *Adult Leadership,* March 1968, 321-338.

Cooper, S.S., and R.S. Lutze. Dial N for Nursing. *Adult Leadership,* December 1970, *19,* 202-203.

Edelman, L. Teaching Adults Via Telelecture and Electrowriter. *Adult Leadership,* October 1968, 164, 189.

Hoyt, D.P., and D.W. Frye. *The Effectiveness of Telecommunications as an Educational Delivery System.* Kansas State University, Manhattan, School of Education, June 1972.

McLuhan, M. *Understanding Media.* London: Routledge and Kegan Paul, 1964.

Parker, L.A. Humanizing Distant Learning Instruction. Paper presented to National Home Study Council, San Diego, California, March 29-30, 1976.

Puzzuoli, D.A. *A Study of Teaching University Extension Classes by Telelecture.* West Virginia University, Morgantown, 1970.

Williams, E., and A. Champanis. A Review of Psychological Research Comparing Communications Media. *The Status of the Telephone in Education.* University of Wisconsin-Extension, May 1976.

V.

DEVELOPMENTAL GUIDE

The first step in preparing for a teleconference is to focus more clearly on the participants and the purpose of the program. By answering a number of questions regarding the clientele group being served and by clarifying the program's purpose, the instructor or program coordinator can go on to make decisions regarding the general presentation style (format) and the type of materials to be prepared. Figure 9 diagrams how that decision-making process might occur.

Description of Clientele

What is their interest in the subject matter? How intense is the interest? Is there an identifiable reason for the interest? In addition, how was existing knowledge acquired? Where would the clientele most likely go for additional information on the subject? What is the level of subject knowledge? What is their general attitude toward the subject under consideration? What are their listening habits?

Clarification of Purpose

What do you wish to accomplish through the teleconferencing program? Is there an interest in simply providing awareness of the subject matter? Is there a certain amount of learning expected? What kind? What should participants do with content after the program? Apply it in their own

Figure 9

Decision-Making Process

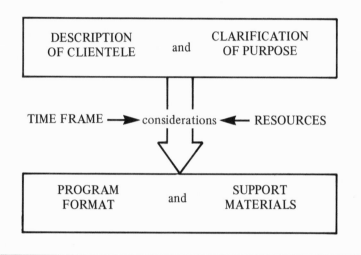

situation? Share it with others? Is it appropriate to expect all participants to achieve the same outcomes?

Time Frame and Resources

When must promotional materials go out? To whom? How? What lead time do local program administrators need? What about registration? If you will be using visuals, when and how many must be reproduced in order to reach the locations in time? When must you have your plans finalized in order for visuals to be made and reproduced? Do you need to send any other materials to the local coordinators? Will you need support staff to work on the program? If so, is there a budget for this? If you are using guests or sharing the work with other faculty, how will you synchronize efforts? Will you be originating from sites other than the central location? Do you need prerecording for backup purposes? What amount of time after the program will be needed for follow-up?

Program Format and Support Materials

How much question-and-answer time is needed? Is there need for discussion time by local groups? What level of subject detail or abstraction should one deal with? What is the logical organization of the content? What are the content limits in terms of time and participants' ability to grasp the main ideas? How much redundance is needed? What are the key ideas? Is there time for summary of key points? Will visuals be used, or other local resources? What print support materials are needed? How much time should be used to introduce the speaker? To humanize? What sources for additional information are available to the participants?

Planning Your Schedule

At this point, after answering questions relevant to the decision-making process, you are ready to get your program from paper into action. Design a plan for yourself with deadlines. Remembering that the first session should be one of the strongest, use the checklist on the following pages (Figures 11, 12, 13, and 14) to incorporate some of the techniques suggested under each of the four steps. (Not all of them will apply to any one program.)

Reference

ETN-SCA-SEEN Dean's Advisory Committee Report. University of Wisconsin-Extension, Madison, 1972.

Figure 11

Developmental Guide Checklist

Teleconference Checklist

Optimum Program Conditions:
Optimum program conditions include advance preparation of participants by sending them a packet of materials containing:
- "welcome-to-the-program" letter
- biographical sketch and picture of the speaker/instructor
- instructions on how to operate the equipment
- topic outline or agenda
- objectives of the teleconference
- selected background reading materials
- highlight questions or summary of major points to be covered

Optimum conditions also include a local facilitating leader at each site to make sure that physical facilities are provided which are conducive to teleconferencing, to welcome participants, and to help them feel comfortable in using the equipment.

General Preparation:
As a general rule, teleconferences should be better planned and organized than in a face-to-face setting. Planning pays off in greater efficiency and satisfaction. The Teleconference Checklist which follows summarizes the four design steps for planning—before, during, and after a teleconference.

Figure 12

Developmental Guide Checklist

Before The Program:

☐ Send out welcome letter with biographical sketch and picture.

☐ Make up roster list from preregistrations (for classes).

☐ Make up and send out "roster information" to group members (for meetings).

☐ Lay out a "cluster circuit" for program origination from other locations.

☐ Plan some personal visits to participants which dovetail with other travel commitments.

Humanizing

☐ Design your participation strategies.

☐ Call several people in advance to ask for "planted questions."

☐ Set up a reactor panel to get discussion ball rolling.

☐ Build participation into printed materials: a list of points or questions to react to, a pre- or post-activity assignment.

☐ Ask for an individual case study or report by arranging ahead.

☐ Plan any group participation formats—buzz group, role-playing.

Participation

☐ Decide how you will cover the material—lecture, discussion, visual presentation.

☐ Decide how much you will present—a rule-of-thumb is three major ideas in 30 minutes.

☐ Plan for variety and short segments. Include an interview, panel discussion, or question-and-answer period.

☐ Prepare printed materials and visuals with enough lead time to send either to individuals or group leaders.

Message Style

☐ Design any written feedback materials—message mailers or feedback forms. Include in advance packets.

☐ Decide if you will do a more formal evaluation and begin planning for this.

Feedback

Figure 13

Developmental Guide Checklist

During The Program:

- ☐ Open the program with an "informal roll call." Welcome group members.
- ☐ Help individuals feel comfortable with teleconferencing equipment.
- ☐ Introduce yourself (and other presenters) informally.
- ☐ Use a natural delivery style; let your personality "come through."
- ☐ Mentally picture and talk to individuals–not to an audience.
- ☐ Ask individuals to identify themselves when they speak; use their names in your responses.
- ☐ Stress meeting individual needs; give a number for phone-in office hours.

Humanizing

- ☐ Plant seeds at the beginning that this is an opportunity to share ideas.
- ☐ Use interactive techniques (case study, role-play, etc.) to get participation.
- ☐ Use questions as a participation tool:
    - *jumping-off questions*
    - *highlight questions*
    - *planted questions*
    - *directive questions (using roster)*
    - *rephrased questions*
- ☐ Ask a group from another location to lead the discussion at times.
- ☐ Divide large groups into buzz groups for discussion purposes.

Participation

- ☐ Use short segments (10-15 minutes). Change activity or voices.
- ☐ Vary pacing. Slower: new or difficult concepts; faster: review and less complex material.
- ☐ Preview-present-review. (The old rule still works: *"Tell them what you're going to tell them, tell them, tell them what you've told them."*)
- ☐ Use printed materials as you go along–get participants to interact with them in some way. (Color-coding or numerical-coding makes this easier to do.)
- ☐ If you use visuals (overhead transparencies or slides), make instructions clear as to which visual is to be projected.

Message Style

(Continued on Next Page)

Figure 13 (Continued)

☐ Be sure to ask for verbal feedback frequently.
☐ You may wish to set "ground rules" for how you want feedback. (Should participants interrupt or will you ask at times for feedback?)
☐ At the end of the program, use a short "Feedback Form" to get a reading on that program's strengths and weaknesses.

Feedback

Figure 14

Developmental Guide Checklist

After The Program:

☐ Be receptive to any requests expressed during the program—try to adapt future programs to meet them, if possible.

☐ Follow-up on any questions that were not answered during the program with a phone call or personal note.

☐ Include individuals as much as possible in planning for future programs—ask them to send you suggestions or phone you.

☐ Keep communication lines open; try to meet with groups or individuals if your travel itinerary permits.

☐ Arrange for groups to meet face-to-face at some time for a half-day conference.

Humanizing

☐ Use a post-activity. Have groups apply what was presented during the program by discussing it at their own locations.

☐ Assign an ongoing project to be done by each individual with a report-back on-the-air at the end of the series.

☐ Ask for individual follow-up in time for the next program, for example, *develop a solution to the problem presented today.* Use a few participants' report as the next program's lead-off.

Participation

☐ Reinforce the major ideas by asking individuals to give themselves a "self-test" by using the list of highlight questions—can they now answer all of the questions on the list?

☐ Use follow-up printed materials for both instructional teleconferences and meetings:

☐ For instructional teleconferences: Send a summary letter to repeat and emphasize major points. This is especially important after a panel discussion.

☐ For meetings: Send a memorandum to list major decisions and/or suggestions made during the program.

Message Style

(Continued on Next Page)

Figure 14 (Continued)

☐ Phone a number of the group leaders from various locations to ask for their impressions of the program.
☐ Listen to the program tape to spot strengths and weaknesses:
- Were individuals made to feel welcome and comfortable with the equipment?
- Were opportunities provided for participation—did individuals take advantage of those opportunities?
- Was the message easy to understand, interestingly presented? What about pacing? Variety?

Feedback

VI.

RESOURCES

ARTICLES

Monson, M. Designing for the Participants. *Journal of Communication,* Summer 1978, *28,*(3).

Parker, L.A., and M. Baird. Humanizing Telephone-Based Instructional Systems. University of Wisconsin-Extension, Madison, 1975.

BOOKS

Monson, M. *Bridging the Distance—Instructional Design for Teleconferencing.* University of Wisconsin-Extension, Madison, 1978.

Parker, L.A., M. Monson, and B. Riccomini. (Eds.) *A Design for Interactive Audio.* University of Wisconsin-Extension, 1977.

Parker, L.A., M. Monson, M. Baird *et al. Teletechniques: Instructional Design for Teleconferencing, A Handbook* (part of workshop materials).

BROCHURE

Monson, M. Designing for Interactive Teleconferencing. University of Wisconsin-Extension, Madison, Wisconsin, 1977.

MEDIA PACKAGE

A media package of videotapes with accompanying print materials describes 12 techniques and how to operationalize them. Called "Twelve Interactive Techniques for Teleconferencing," it focuses on such formats as case study, role-play, question-and-answer periods, and reactor panels suggesting ways to adapt them to teleconferencing.

WORKSHOPS

The Center for Interactive Programs (CIP) at the University of Wisconsin-Extension, Madison, Wisconsin, home of the Educational Telephone Network (ETN), sponsors workshops on a number of topics relating to teleconferencing. Instructional design for teleconferencing is the focus of at least one seminar annually.

IN USE

The Teletechniques workshop and training program is in use at the Educational Telephone Network (ETN) at the University of Wisconsin-Extension, Madison, Wisconsin. Other teleconferencing networks across the United States and Canada have adapted portions of the Teletechniques training program and design model for use in their own systems.

DIRECTORY OF SYSTEMS

For a directory of teleconferencing systems currently operational in the world, contact: Newsletter Editor, Center for Interactive Programs, University of Wisconsin-Extension, Madison, Wisconsin.

LORNE A. PARKER is Director of Instructional Communications Systems at the University of Wisconsin-Extension. In this capacity, he heads three major statewide communications systems designed to provide continuing education for students throughout the state of Wisconsin. A member of the University of Wisconsin-Extension faculty for the past 14 years, Dr. Parker played a significant role in the development and operation of new University of Wisconsin-Extension communications systems designed to take education to the people. He did his doctoral research in mass communications and adult education, with specific focus on compressed speech, at the University of Wisconsin. Dr. Parker is the author of several books, including *The Telephone in Education, Book II* and *A Design for Interactive Audio.* He has also written numerous articles for professional journals and provided consultation work for major educational and electronic manufacturers.

MAVIS K. MONSON, a member of the University of Wisconsin-Extension faculty, works in the area of instructional design for teleconferencing programs. She advises programmers who use the teleconferencing networks administered by Instructional Communications Systems (ICS). In that capacity, she consults with faculty who use either the Educational Telephone Network (ETN), which is an audio system, or the Statewide Extension Educational Network (SEEN), which is an audio system with telewriting capability. Continually researching those teaching techniques which facilitate effective teleconference programs, she has developed the *Teletechniques* workshop, one of the first comprehensive training programs to help people in the design, implementation, and evaluation of teleconferencing. This program is not only used by Wisconsin faculty but also has been adopted by many systems in the U.S. and Canada.